More Good Words for
The Art of Transformational Leadership

"No matter where you find yourself, in a king's palace or in a large corporation or a family, Mark McCloskey and Jim Louwsma show you how to make a significant positive difference both in the lives of the people you're leading and in the outcomes you're pursuing."

ANDREA BUCZYNSKI
Vice President Global Leadership
Development/HR—Cru

"The 4-R Model changed my life and leadership. It's a user-friendly diagnostic tool that readily gets you on the solution side of problems. It's a leadership compass that helps you know where to go and how to get there. I use it every day in my personal life and corporate community. It transforms how you lead and the lives you influence."

JOEL JOHNSON
Senior Pastor—Westwood Community Church

"If you need to build a culture that both matters and has staying power, read this book! Jim and Mark have captured the essence of how being a transformational leader is today's best way forward using relevant lessons from our past. It is inspiring and timely reading for enlightened leaders."

JOE MARZANO
President and CEO—Martius Group LLC

The Art of Virtue-Based
Transformational
Leadership

Building Strong Businesses, Organizations and Families

Mark McCloskey
Jim Louwsma

with Dave Aeilts

Cover and Interior Design: The Dugan Design Group
www.thedugandesigngroup.com

Editor: Grace Smith
grace.j.smith@gmail.com

Printed in the United States of America.

ISBN 978-0-9887356-2-0

Library of Congress Catalog Number 2014933292

Published by: The Wordsmith
P.O. Box 385168
Bloomington, Minnesota 55438
daeilts@comcast.net

TABLE OF CONTENTS

Preface:
Big L or Little l Leaders

E veryone has leadership potential. Some of us are big **L** leaders, presiding over large organizations with thousands of employees and constituents. Many of us, on the other hand, are little **l** leaders. We have accepted responsibility for leadership in small businesses, our local communities, and our families. At some point in life, every one of us will face the choice to do something about a problem—or to do nothing. That's a call to leadership.

We teach a course in the MBA program at Bethel University, St. Paul, Minnesota. At the beginning of the course, we ask our students, "How many of you are leaders?" Typically, only one or two raise their hands. At the end of the course, we ask the same question: "How many of you are leaders?" Every hand goes up. What changed? Simply this: all of the students have come to understand they have an opportunity to make a difference in their own sphere of influence, however limited or expansive.

Big **L** or little **l.** Both are important. Which are you?

Introduction:
A Thirst for Real Leaders

S troll the business aisle of your local bookstore, or take a virtual stroll of
booksellers on the Internet. You will soon conclude that leadership is a
hot topic. In the first decade of this new century, hundreds of volumes and
countless journal articles, websites, and blogs addressing the topic of leadership development and practice have flooded the market. This proliferation
of writings on leadership is driven by three factors:

- Concern for the effectiveness of American business enterprises
  and public institutions, given the increasingly rapid rate of change.

- Concern for America's capacity to compete economically in a
  hyper-competitive world economy.

- Concern about the quality of life after decades of moral erosion
  and loss of community consensus on core values.

Based on the sheer volume of leadership writings, we might erro-
neously conclude that these concerns have been adequately addressed—
that America is a land rich in leaders. But the quantity of our leadership
resources in no way reflects the quality of our leadership. We seem to be
drowning in information about leadership but lacking the intellectual and
moral capacity to synthesize and apply this information.

Far too many of our contemporary leaders are dedicated to personal
ascendancy at the expense of public trust. Too many leaders willingly sacrifice integrity and public credibility on the altars of personal pleasure and
preservation of power. Too many have adopted self-serving agendas that
exploit followers for personal gain.

Our nation cannot distinguish between talent and character, or between celebrities and leaders. Not surprisingly, our public institutions, from business and government to our non-profit organizations and families, are increasingly characterized by cynicism, lack of vision and fractured relationships—all symptoms of leaderlessness.

Leadership v. Management

What is a real leader? Millions called Hitler, Stalin, and Mao their leaders; but if they only followed on threat of imprisonment or at gunpoint, that's not leadership. I'm sure you agree. In America, poor leadership often manifests itself in abuse of power and position. Just because someone has a title doesn't make that person a leader. We've all seen the damage so-called "leaders" have wrought on organizations and people in those organizations. Consider Enron and its long-time employees who lost their retirement savings and hope for the future because of the fraudulent financial dealings of Ken Lay and Jeff Skillings.

Real leaders, whether big **L** or little **l**, can bless their followers, and those impersonating leaders can be a real curse.

Many confuse leadership with management. Strong organizations need good managers and good leaders. Both are important. Some use these terms interchangeably, but there is a difference.

Management entails planning and budgeting, organizing and staffing, controlling and problem solving, predictability and order. It is primarily focused on running the business of the organization for today versus looking into the future.

General Motors is an example of an organization that was well managed but poorly led. Failing to consistently face the demands of reality, GM eventually stumbled into bankruptcy, costing its employees and stockholders much financial pain, not to mention the taxpayers who had to pay for the government bailout.

Leadership, on the other hand, is all about establishing direction, casting a vision, developing strategy, and aligning people to the direction of that vision and strategy.

Historians speak with great admiration of Sir Ernest Shackleton who in 1914 led an expedition with the goal of being the first to cross the continent of Antarctica. His was a noble aspiration during this final age of exploration.

Shackleton placed the following ad in London newspapers: "Men wanted for hazardous journey. Small wages, bitter cold, long months of complete darkness, constant danger, safe return doubtful. Honour and recognition in case of success." Undeterred by its dire warnings, the ad attracted thousands of would-be explorers from whom Shackleton chose twenty-five for his crew.

True, England had fallen on hard financial times, but its people also hungered for a cause greater than self-interest. They showed a willingness to follow a leader's vision and strategy, despite the odds.

Real leaders motivate and inspire people to become engaged and to go the extra mile in service of a noble cause. They generate substantive and often dramatic change that transforms organizations and the individuals in them.

> **The expedition's ship, Endurance, broke up in an ice flow forcing the crew to endure all manner of dangers and hardship. While failing to achieve the initial goal, Shackleton is widely acclaimed for extraordinary leadership that resulted in each and every member of his crew returning home alive.**

Transformational v. Transactional Leadership

Contemporary theorists distinguish between two broad approaches to leadership practice: *transactional* and *transformational*.

The relationships of most leaders and followers are transactional in nature. *The transactional leader seeks to make a deal* that will appeal to the self-interest of both leader and follower. The result is usually an exchange based on the wants or needs of the two parties. For instance, a candidate for public office may promise lower taxes in exchange for a citizen's vote. In business, a manager may offer a weekly paycheck in exchange for forty hours of work.

Wants and needs of leaders and followers in a transactional relationship are usually different from one another. Of transactional relationships, leadership author and theorist James MacGregor Burns writes, "The object in these cases is not a joint effort for persons with common aims acting for the collective interests of followers, but a bargain to aid the individual interests of persons or groups going their separate ways."

By contrast, the transformational leader seeks to engage followers in a relationship based on their mutual commitment to a set of values, a mission, or a vision of a better future. The result binds leaders and followers together in a mutually uplifting partnership in which they inspire and motivate one another.

Transformational leaders create and clearly communicate agendas for moral, ethical, and spiritual change that lift people out of their everyday concerns. Whatever separate interests they hold, the transformational leader forges consensus among followers in pursuit of a better future worthy of the best efforts of both leader and follower. As a result, both the individual and the organization moves from an undesirable present to a better future…or from a good today to a great tomorrow.

Transactional and transformational leadership styles may be further distinguished by exploring the difference between a contract and a covenant.

- *A contract* clarifies expectations and obligations between two parties. It spells out the quid pro quo (this for that) of any engagement. Transactional leadership, based on exchange, is essentially contractual in nature. There is nothing wrong with that. We need contracts to manage our expectations and to structure our interactions so we and others do what we promise. But we want and need more out of life. Contracts are limited in scope and time, and the exchange involved is usually not personal. There is nothing lasting about this temporary relationship. As human beings, we desire covenants.

- *A covenant* is a heart-felt pledge to honor and stay true to one another over long periods of time. Covenants fulfill deep human needs to connect, to belong, and to care for one another in genuine, lasting relationships. In the organizational context, covenants apply to something beyond self-interest, like a meaningful cause. They bind us together in mutual service. Transformational leadership is essentially covenantal in nature. Leaders and followers engage in a shared purpose and common destiny—connected to something larger than the work of any given day or the contractual obligations of any given task.

This book champions a transformational model of leadership. We contend that transactional leadership is inadequate to deal with the fundamental challenges facing our institutions, public and private, in the twenty-first century. By contrast, transformational leadership builds up followers.

While, contrary to popular terminology, transformational leaders don't "empower" anyone, they do release the energy, strength and gifting others already possess. Transformational leaders serve as catalysts to help others recognize their God-given assets—what God has already entrusted to them and is developing within them—and to identify ways to put these assets to use as good stewards in the service of others.

In this, transformational leadership provides not only the ethical foundation but also the personal and spiritual motivation for meeting these challenges. You can play a part in restoring hope to a leaderless world. Whether big **L** or little **l**, this book was written for you.

Anyone Can Lead

The debate continues over whether leaders are born or made. Proponents of the contemporary Great Man Theory contend that certain people are endowed from birth with "the right stuff" for leadership. On the other hand, history is replete with examples of common people who took up the mantle of leadership and accomplished great things.

You can play a part in restoring hope to a leaderless world.

In the Prologue, you will meet a man named Nehemiah who walked this earth 2,500 years ago. He left a memoir describing an incredible feat accomplished by a group of poor, downtrodden ex-slaves which he led.

We have no record that Nehemiah was particularly adept at leadership. He had an important role in the royal court of Persia, which may have given him access to education and obviously provided him a significant life experience. However, we do not find anything in his portfolio that indicates he was a great man, charismatic, or destined to lead.

Nehemiah served as cupbearer to the king of Persia. As such, he tasted everything before the king consumed it, so apparently he was trustworthy. What Nehemiah seems to have had going for him was his virtuous character.

We believe anyone can learn to lead. It may be easier for some than for others, and a few may decline the opportunity. But for those who aspire to leadership and for the many required to lead by circumstance or by calling, this book offers a roadmap to follow. Let's get started on the journey.

Mark McCloskey   Jim Louwsma

Authors' Note: For the most part, this book cites both ancient and recent historical examples of transformational leadership. While contemporary exemplars of transformational virtues continue to make a difference in our world, the authors hesitate to cite them since their lives are not yet finished. Not all who begin well end well. For this reason, the majority of exemplars mentioned herein lived out these virtues to the end of their days.

Leadership: One Word, Two Brands

TRANSACTIONAL	TRANSFORMATIONAL
Exchange	Engagement
Contract	Covenant
Renters	Owners
Task	Vision
Control	Empowerment
Program	Strategies
Organize	Align
Incentives	Inspiration
Job Finished	People Changed

Artist's concept of Jerusalem walls in Nehemiah's day.   Reconstruction © Leen Ritmeye

Prologue

Nehemiah: An Unlikely Leader

The historical writings of the ancient Israelites contain a towering example of leadership. A man named Nehemiah, revered by two world religions, played the central role in a drama that unfolded 2,500 years ago in the old city of Susa. Located near present-day Shush in western Iran, Susa served as a winter residence for Persian royalty. Nehemiah's autobiographical story appears in the Old Testament book bearing his name.

The story begins in 445 BC when Nehemiah, a Jewish exile, worked as cupbearer to the most powerful man on the globe: Artaxerxes I, King of Persia.

One hundred and forty-two years earlier, the Babylonians had conquered Nehemiah's ancestors. The invaders decimated Israel's capital city, Jerusalem. They destroyed the Jewish temple, the center of their community life, and carried off its gold and silver vessels. They burned the city's gates and demolished its walls. They killed thousands and forced thousands more to march to Babylon as slaves. The invaders left only the poorest of the poor to eke out a living in rural areas surrounding the ravaged city.

Both Jews and Christians embrace The Book of Nehemiah.

Thirty years later, the Persians overthrew the Babylonians and became the most significant force in the world. The Persians had a more benevolent attitude toward conquered peoples. They allowed them to return to their homelands if they wished. In 536 BC around fifty thousand Jews who had been born in captivity returned to Jerusalem. They found the city with no walls for security, no temple, and a despairing population oppressed by local tribes. An atmosphere of brokenness and hopelessness pervaded the ruins.

The returning Jews began rebuilding their temple and completed it in 515 BC. In 459 BC they attempted to rebuild the city walls. But their enemies sent letters to King Artaxerxes, accusing them of treason. That put an end to the reconstruction.

Fourteen years later, Nehemiah entered the picture. A valued servant in the royal court, he petitioned the king for permission to travel eight hundred miles (a four-month journey) to his ancestral home to look after his people's welfare and serve as governor of the Province of Judah. The king graciously approved this request. Soon after Nehemiah arrived on the scene and despite fierce opposition, the former cupbearer led the down-trodden residents of Jerusalem in rebuilding and restoring (in an astounding fifty-two days) the city's gates and miles of walls that had lain in ruin for 142 years. Most significantly, Nehemiah's leadership restored the morale and community of this defeated people.

Though ancient in its setting, Nehemiah's story has powerful relevance in today's world. We live at a time when broken-down walls abound, literally and figuratively. With low morale and disengaged workers, organizations flounder. A sense of hopelessness pervades, not just in the workplace but in our families and communities. We need leaders like Nehemiah with the ability to transform our despair to hope and our brokenness to something new. We must not only rebuild our institutions, but also restore life and hope to the communities within their walls.

In the chapters that follow, we will examine Nehemiah as an example of leadership that blesses and transforms those being led. We'll introduce a model to help you picture this approach to leadership, and we'll highlight individuals and organizations whose leadership builds and transforms. Whether you are a big **L** or a little **l** leader, you will be challenged and equipped to lead like Nehemiah.

1

Transformational Leadership: What does it look like?

The Ancient Text–The Book of Nehemiah 1:1-10

¹ These are the memoirs of Nehemiah son of Hacaliah.

Nehemiah's Concern for Jerusalem

In late autumn, in the month of Kislev, in the twentieth year of King Artaxerxes' reign, I was at the fortress of Susa. ² Hanani, one of my brothers, came to visit me with some other men who had just arrived from Judah. I asked them about the Jews who had returned there from captivity and about how things were going in Jerusalem.

³ They said to me, "Things are not going well for those who returned to the province of Judah. They are in great trouble and disgrace. The wall of Jerusalem has been torn down, and the gates have been destroyed by fire."

⁴ When I heard this, I sat down and wept. In fact, for days I mourned, fasted, and prayed to the God of heaven. ⁵ Then I said,

"O LORD, God of heaven, the great and awesome God who keeps his covenant of unfailing love with those who love him and obey his commands, ⁶ listen to my prayer! Look down and see me praying night and day for your people Israel. I confess

that we have sinned against you. Yes, even my own family and I have sinned! [7] *We have sinned terribly by not obeying the commands, decrees, and regulations that you gave us through your servant Moses.*

[8] *"Please remember what you told your servant Moses: 'If you are unfaithful to me, I will scatter you among the nations.* [9] *But if you return to me and obey my commands and live by them, then even if you are exiled to the ends of the earth, I will bring you back to the place I have chosen for my name to be honored.'*

[10] *"The people you rescued by your great power and strong hand are your servants.* [11] *O Lord, please hear my prayer! Listen to the prayers of those of us who delight in honoring you. Please grant me success today by making the king favorable to me. Put it into his heart to be kind to me."*

In those days I was the king's cup-bearer.

To the Reader: *A story that is 2,500 years old requires some background for the modern reader to grasp. Immediately after each installment of Nehemiah's autobiography, you will find a section entitled "Nehemiah's Story Updated." This is a fictional but plausible account of a Jewish writer we will call Jotham. Jotham's eye-witness account of Nehemiah's adventures will help clarify the ancient text.*

Nehemiah's Story Updated

Soon after Nehemiah became cupbearer to the king, a young journalist named Jotham was assigned to cover the day-to-day activities of the royal court. Over the years, the two men became friends. Here is Jotham's version of the Nehemiah's story.

One day in 444 BC, Jotham met Nehemiah outside the palace and noticed a change in his friend's appearance. The cupbearer was clothed in rough burlap, instead of the fine linen garments he usually wore, and smudges of charcoal streaked his forehead. Noticeably absent was the usual cheery expression on Nehemiah's face. "What's the matter?" asked Jotham.

"About a year ago, my brother Hanani joined a caravan bound for Judah," said Nehemiah sadly. "He hoped to start a business in Jerusalem where our great-grandparents lived. It had been ninety years since many of our people returned to Judah, so my brother assumed the city would be flourishing."

Then Nehemiah explained his long face. "My brother has just returned with heart-breaking news," he told Jotham. "Instead of finding Jerusalem abuzz with activity and promise, he saw that the city walls are still in ruins and our people are being treated like second-class citizens by trespassers and interlopers with no legal right to the land."

"But Nehemiah," countered Jotham. "Your great-grandparents are dead and your family lives in Susa now. Besides, you have a cushy job in the king's palace—why worry about a ruined city you have never even visited?"

"Long before we were cupbearers and reporters, we were Israelites," Nehemiah replied. "Those are our people, our extended family, who are disgraced and in trouble in that faraway land." Then Nehemiah reminded his friend that the God they both worshipped had promised to restore the Jews to their homeland at some point in the future.

"I believe it's time," said Nehemiah, his sad face transforming into a smile. "I've been made a cupbearer for a purpose larger than my own interests, and perhaps you have the job of court reporter for the same reason." Nehemiah paused and then confided in Jotham, "I've decided to ask the king to help us restore the city of our ancestors."

"But," protested Jotham, "you know that King Artaxerxes is the one who stopped Jerusalem's residents from rebuilding the city wall a few years back. Why risk his wrath and your own position by bringing the subject up again?"

"Because, if I do not put my livelihood and even my life at risk," said Nehemiah with a determined look, "who in lesser circumstances will dare to jeopardize what they have to secure a better future for us all." Paraphrasing the words spoken of a Jewish Queen who had risen to prominence before an earlier Persian king, Nehemiah mused, "Who knows but that I have come to my current favored position for such a time as this."

Jotham shook his head in disbelief.

Marks of a Transformational Leader

Transformational leaders create and articulate agendas for moral, ethical and spiritual change that lift people out of their everyday affairs and ordinary selves. Whatever separate interests are held, the transformational leader forges consensus among followers in pursuit of a future worthy of everyone's best efforts. Nehemiah was such a leader.

Five marks characterize transformational leaders (TFLs):

- TFLs function as effective agents of personal and corporate change.

- TFLs are themselves caught up in the transformational process.

- TFLs serve the best and highest interests of others.

- TFLs create and sustain healthy organizations and communities by imparting hope and forging mutual partnerships.

- TFLs prepare the next generation of leaders.

Look closer at how Nehemiah exhibited each of these characteristics.

TFLs function as effective agents of personal and corporate change. Transformational leaders act as catalysts for empowering personal change in their follower's lives and for holding them accountable to operate at their best. Followers change from renters into owners, from spectators into voluntarily and sacrificially engaged participants, and from people locked in self-interest to people willing to sacrifice for the interests of others. *See Renters v. Owners on page 32.*

Nehemiah's leadership transformed Jerusalem's self-interested, spectator-residents into people willing to sacrifice for the sake of rebuilding the wall. Farmers literally abandoned their crops in the fields and those in the city left their occupations to join Nehemiah in the fifty-two-day wall-building effort. He lifted the dispirited Jews out of their despair and despondency, helping them to become a secure community and restoring their national confidence. Jerusalem was the heart of the land God had promised to his people. The rebuilding of its walls symbolized the restoration of their relationship with God and gave them hope.

Transformational leaders also serve as a catalyst for substantive corporate change, in keeping with the vision and values of the organization—be it a business, a non-profit association, or a family. That which is unacceptable in the status quo is eliminated (or at least changed over time) and a desirable future is ushered in.

By rebuilding its walls, Nehemiah transformed Jerusalem from a state of insecurity to a city brimming with confidence. Once their enemies were outside, the Jews could begin restoring their community and living out their core values.

TFLs are themselves caught up in the transformational process. As a catalyst for substantive and lasting change, transformational leaders undergo the same change they envision for those they lead. "Be the change that you wish to see in the world," urged Mahatma Gandhi, pointing out the need for real leaders to embody the values and vision they advocate.

In Chapter 1 of his memoirs, Nehemiah aligned himself with the vision God had given to Moses centuries earlier. Responding to that vision, Nehemiah included himself in a confession of Israel's sins, reminded God of his promise to bring them back from exile, and asked for his blessing, personally and corporately. As such, Nehemiah could walk into Jerusalem, a living embodiment of that promise—not perfect, but substantially reflecting the vision and values of God. To bring about transformation, Nehemiah recognized that he, also, must undergo transformation.

TFLs serve the best and highest interests of others. They've settled in their hearts and minds issues of power and self-esteem to the degree that they are able to empower others and seek their welfare. They're not using their position to feed some emotional deficit. Rather than creating power for themselves, they're healthy enough to give away power and to genuinely delegate responsibility.

Nehemiah had a very good position as cupbearer to the king. Not only that, but he was seven generations removed from the fall of Jerusalem. Nehemiah had every reason not to give up the power and comforts his position afforded and travel eight hundred miles west of Susa to a city he had never seen. He had no assurance the people of that city would receive him or that he'd be successful. But he was willing to give all that up to serve others. At his own expense, he took personal responsibility for a public need. Nehemiah put his vision from God above his own security and made the initial sacrifice before asking others to do so.

TFLs create and sustain healthy communities by imparting hope and forging mutual partnerships. Transformational leaders deeply believe and passionately communicate that a better future is on the horizon. "The self-sacrifice involved in mutual sharing and cooperative action is impossible without hope," says American moral and social philosopher Eric Hoffer. "When today is all there is, we grab all we can and hold on. On the other hand, when everything is ahead and yet to come, we find it easy to share all we have and to forgo advantages within our grasp."

Nehemiah knew from his study of Moses' writings that God was not finished with the nation of Israel. Better years—years of restoration and service—were ahead. His hope was not a matter of positive thinking but rather was grounded in God's word.

Successful, sustained, healthy, community-building change also requires mutual partnerships. Transformational leaders must have the capacity to initiate and sustain such relationships with partners whose voluntary and wholehearted involvement in the vision is necessary for its success.

> **The ultimate test of a transformational leader is the ability to raise up a new generation of leaders to strengthen and expand the community.**

As we will see in coming chapters, Nehemiah entered into a diverse array of healthy and transforming relationships—first with the king and the commanders of his army, and then with the residents of Jerusalem, both common people and community leaders. All found it in their best interests to forge an enduring partnership with Nehemiah. By imparting hope, he elevated the motivations, aspirations, and competencies of these men and women who were better off for having been in partnership with him and with one another.

TFLs prepare the next generations of leaders. The test of a transformational leader is not the completion of tasks or even the development of followers. The ultimate test of transformational leadership is the reproduction of a new generation of transformational leaders to strengthen and expand the transformational community. Substantial, healthy, and healing change will not last apart from the work of the next generation of leaders. Transformation is never finished.

Nehemiah, properly concerned for the lasting legacy of his reforms, focused the latter part of his career on seeking to institutionalize the changes he made earlier. Under his direction and in concert with other leaders, Nehemiah established centers for the training of a new generation of leaders. At the end of his career, the battle for the hearts and minds of the restored community still raged on.

The battle to sustain healthy change across generations continues. The transformational organization—whether business, community or family—is only one generation from extinction, or worse, irrelevance. A new generation of leaders must be prepared for responsibilities and opportunities on and over the horizon. Consequently, transformational leaders do not aim to develop docile followers who fit the mold. While consistent in the values they embrace, the next generation of leaders may lead in a manner and style different from that of the original leaders who empowered them.

Joshua Chamberlain: A Transformational Leader

Joshua Lawrence Chamberlain, a hero of the American Civil War, serves as a stirring example of what transformational leadership looks like. Born in 1828 in Brewer, Maine to a military family, the young Chamberlain chose a more peaceful career path. He excelled in academics and graduated from Bowdoin College, Brunswick, Maine, in 1852. After additional schooling, Chamberlain secured a position teaching modern languages at his alma mater in 1855.

When the Civil War broke out, Chamberlain's revulsion at slavery overtook his devotion to academics and compelled him to enlist in the Union Army. In 1862 he was commissioned by the governor as a lieutenant colonel in the Twentieth Maine Regiment. With no prior military training, Chamberlain learned the craft of war as he had ancient Greek—through diligent study. Nine months later, the army promoted him to full colonel.

During the war, Chamberlain led Union soldiers in many major battles. As a result of his determination to join his men in the thick of the fighting, he also suffered six wounds. But the conflict for which this professor-turned-soldier received greatest acclaim was the Battle of Little Round Top, part of the larger Battle of Gettysburg. Down to a third of the regiment's original strength and with ammunition running low, Chamberlain initiated a brilliant bayonet charge that routed the Confederate soldiers seeking to overrun his position. Some say this thirty-four-year-old saved the Union Army from defeat in this critical battle and in so doing changed the course of the war. For his heroic leadership at Little Round Top, Chamberlain received the Congressional Medal of Honor. For his continued bravery and heroism throughout the remainder of the war, Chamberlain was chosen by Ulysses S. Grant to receive the Confederate Army's surrender at Appomattox.

But Chamberlain's leadership extended beyond brilliant military strategy and his rank as an officer. He projected values and a vision for a better tomorrow that his men embraced. He appealed to their common heritage as Maine volunteers and their shared desire to see the country reunited, without the disgrace of slavery.

That Chamberlain's Twentieth Maine Regiment played a pivotal role in the Battle of Gettysburg is undisputed. They held out against tremendous odds and kept the Union line from being overrun and collapsing. Less well-known is that about a third of the 360 Maine volunteers fighting that day were deserters from the Second Maine, which had been disbanded. They had headed home without permission from their commanding officer. Another army unit had rounded them up and brought them as mutineers to Chamberlain before the Battle of Gettysburg. Chamberlain was told he could shoot them if they did not fight. Instead, the professor-colonel dismissed the captors, fed the 120 deserters, and sat them down for a talk.

"I've been ordered to take you men with me," Chamberlain informed the deserters in *The Killer Angels*, a civil war novel praised for its realism. "I've been told that if you don't come I can shoot you—well, you know I won't do that. Not Maine men," he vowed. "I won't shoot any man who doesn't want this fight."

That settled, Chamberlain appealed to their common heritage and shared vision of a land where all men, whether black or white, are free. According to *Killer Angels*, he concluded his remarks with a clear assessment of the risk and once again put the decision in their hands. "We're down below half strength and we need you, no doubt of that," said the young colonel. "But whether you fight or not is up to you." In the end, 114 of the 120 deserters chose to follow Chamberlain into battle. They and the remaining soldiers of the Twentieth

Maine held off a Confederate army that far outnumbered them.

In his role as a Union officer, as in private life, Chamberlain exhibited the marks of a transformational leader. He not only advocated for change from the college lectern, but also led others in their pursuit of a better future by investing himself in the effort. By displaying personal confidence in their purpose and by executing strategic decisions in time of crisis, Chamberlain guided his men to victory against overwhelming odds. *TFLs function as effective agents of personal and corporate change.*

By first speaking in favor of the Union Army's cause and then enlisting when he could have languished in the relative safety of his teaching position, Chamberlain pronounced his willingness to undergo the same change he envisioned for those he would lead. *TFLs are themselves caught up in the transformational process.*

Despite decimation of the ranks from casualties, illness and desertion, the professor kept 360 men focused on a purpose bigger than their self-interests—cessation of slavery and the reunion of the country. *TFLs create and sustain healthy communities by imparting hope and forging mutual partnerships.*

Chamberlain personally participated in the battle. Putting himself in harm's way, he strode back and forth along the battle line, encouraging and repositioning his men as waves of Confederate soldiers broke against their ranks. *TFLs serve the best and highest interests of others.*

Marks of a Transformational Organization

In the same way leaders show themselves to be transformational by what they do, organizations running on transformational principles exhibit characteristics that set them apart. Whether for-profits, non-for-profits, or even families, these groups display their transformational nature by the way their leaders and their people conduct business.

Many organizations adopt vision, mission, or values statements, but few walk the talk. Those who do, have the potential to bring about substantive and lasting change in their markets, their communities, and their world.

Below are four marks of genuinely transformational organizations (TOs):

- TOs hold and daily reinforce deep-rooted values.

- Leaders of TOs are deeply committed to their people.

- The people of TOs are engaged.

- TOs lean into the future.

TOs hold and daily reinforce deep-rooted values. Transformational organizations are not perfect in everything they do, but they honor their values, refer to them in every decision, and stand behind them at all costs. Moreover, they spend resources and time building those values into their people and culture. This effort results in a very clear sense of direction, and progress in that direction may be easily detected.

Leaders of TOs are deeply committed to their people. The people are, in reality, a transformational organization's most important asset. It is not just a buzzword. Leaders of transformational organizations serve the employees or members of the organization, not the other way around. Leaders are genuinely collaborative and focused on developing the next generation of leaders.

The people of TOs are engaged. Employees or members of a transformational organization enter into a covenant relationship with the organization (and with each other) to live by its principles. As a result, they take ownership of the organization, its purpose and values, and the contribution they have been asked to make. Through mutual interdependence, leaders and followers make each other better along the way.

TOs lean into the future. TOs realize that true transformation is an on-going process. As noted earlier, any organization is just one generation away from extinction. So the vision is never fully accomplished. The more things change, the greater the need to change in concert with the organization's values. Genuine transformational organizations recognize the enormity of this truth and always feel one step behind.

In the chapters to come, you will notice examples of transformational organizations. Be advised! Transformational organizations, like transformational leaders, are not perfect; however, a genuinely transformational company is in the process of addressing integrity issues in a meaningful way. If there is a gap between its stated values and its behavior, the organization will candidly face up to it, deal with it, and move forward. That is a sure sign of both a transformational leader and a transformational organization.

The most effective leaders and organizations live in a state of constant improvement, which means success at any given moment is not guaranteed, and the possibility of failure at any given moment is not eliminated, according to Henry Cloud, author and leadership consultant. Cloud contends that integrity has nothing to do with perfection but everything to do with candor and honesty around the demands of reality.

A transformational organization may stray from its values, but if these values are woven in the fabric of its culture, the organization will come back to them—unless they have not been passed down to the next generation.

Procter & Gamble: A Transformational Company

I (Jim) was privileged to work for Procter and Gamble (P&G) for almost thirty years. This multi-national company was, and is, one of the world's leading producers of consumer goods. It owns hundreds of brands like Tide, Charmin, Crest, Bounty and others. Most of these brands rank number one or two in their sales categories. Ninety-five percent of U.S. households have at least one P&G branded product in their home.

P&G is as close to a transformational company as any organization I have observed. I never felt like I "just had a job" at P&G. I always felt I had an important responsibility to the company and to those with whom I worked. I left P&G a stronger, wiser, and better person than when I began.

P&G was always leaning into the future, trying to lead and continually improve every phase of its operations, yet the company was anchored by a strong purpose, a set of values, and principles. The Purpose, Value, and Principles (PVP) statement was a living document. It guided every decision we made. *See Procter & Gamble's PVP on page 33.*

I learned the PVP my first day at P&G. The statement was

continually referred to during my career and reinforced, usually in stories, by my leaders. As I grew in my experience and leadership responsibilities, I reinforced the PVP with those I supervised.

One incident early in my career with P&G ingrained in me the importance and privilege of being associated with a company that does what it says it will do. I was selling a feminine hygiene product called Rely. It was a terrific product that was rapidly gaining the dominant share in its category. Then the Center for Disease Control released a study concluding that Rely might cause "toxic shock syndrome" in some women. Shortly after this study was released, our CEO made the decision to pull the Rely brand off the market.

I was stunned. Why would we pull a game-changing product like Rely from the retail store shelves, at least without a fight? Others asked the same questions. Our CEO reminded us that our PVP stated, "We will provide branded products and services of superior quality and value that improve the lives of the world's consumers." If there was a chance it could cause harm, even in a handful of cases, Rely was not improving the lives of consumers; therefore, the only right thing to do was to pull it off the market. That made a tremendous impression on me. My company "walked the talk" regarding its values.

I spent almost three decades with P&G and witnessed innumerable examples of living out our values and principles. For example, one principle states: "The interests of the company and the individual are inseparable." Over and over I saw the company make decisions that benefitted the individual employee or customer. As a result, I continually felt a real sense of ownership that led to a desire to add value every day to the company and those with whom I worked.

The clarity and importance around our Purpose, Values, and Principles grounded everything we did and is one of the big reasons P&G has been around for 175 years. The company's values anchored it during the storms of war, through multiple recessions and a depression, and across decades of political and social change. That is not to suggest everything always went smoothly or right, but our PVP gave us a compass to ride out the storms.

Transformational Leaders Needed

The blistering rate of change, the uncertainty of a global economy, and the loss of integrity from Main Street to Wall Street plead for an approach to leadership that sets a higher bar than the transactional leadership styles in practice today. America—indeed, the world—hungers for transformational leaders.

Gallup studied businesses in the U.S. to determine employee engagement levels in the workforce. The study found 55% of the workforce was disengaged and another 16% was actively disengaged. Disengaged workers are a huge cost to any organization, and actively disengaged workers can actually do damage to the organization's mission. The same study found that 29% of the workforce was actively engaged. These employees got up every morning asking, "How can I drive this business forward?" These workers "owned" the values and vision of their companies.

Transformational leaders engage their followers. These leaders act as catalysts for empowering personal change in their followers' lives. In turn, the followers seek to improve their organization by investing time and talents out of deep conviction that their mutual efforts will result in a substantially brighter future.

Transformational leaders shine in situations where reform is required. They are especially effective in inspiring people who have previously settled for minimal involvement and a low ceiling of achievement to work sacrificially for change that benefits everyone.

Transformational leaders serve. Their followers willingly make sacrifices because transformational leaders serve as they lead. In a transactional leadership model, the follower serves the leader. Transformational leadership flips that principle upside down as leaders serve followers. Nehemiah, on whose example this book is based, served as he led and led as he served; he did so in the context of bringing about lasting change to Jerusalem.

In coming chapters, we will introduce you to a virtue-based, working model of transformational leadership called The 4-R Model. The 4-R Model offers a theoretically sound, conceptually simple, and practical framework for understanding team leadership in a global context. These principles may be applied by big **L** or little **l** leaders to any size or structure of public or private organization.

We are not suggesting that any leadership model can be labeled purely transformational. Transactions are an important factor in any organization, from the company which fairly compensates its workers to parents who agree on the appropriate compensation for a child willing to mow the lawn. But if leadership is only transactional, leaders or organizations are limited in what they can achieve. The 4-R Model of Transformational Leadership provides a higher ceiling for accomplishment. Today's leadership challenges, from the corporate conference table to the family dinner table, demand that higher ceiling.

GAINING PERSONAL PERSPECTIVE

Economist and political philosopher Thomas Sowell states, "Visions are the silent shapers of our thought." If this is true, it is vitally important that we get in touch with the shapers of our vision—our driving passions.

Nehemiah's passion stemmed from a promise God made to bring the exiles home. What are you passionate about? What or who has captured your heart?

_____

_____

Are you a renter or an owner? _____

What would inspire you to work and live sacrificially, foregoing immediate self-interest for a higher cause?

_____

_____

Who do you know, whether little l or big L, that exhibits the marks of transformational leaders like Nehemiah or Chamberlain? What about them is attractive?

_____

_____

Procter & Gamble's Purpose, Values, and Principles

PURPOSE

We will provide branded products and services of superior quality and value that improve the lives of the world's consumers.

As a result, consumers will reward us with leadership sales, profit and value creation, allowing our people, our shareholders, and the communities in which we live and work to prosper.

VALUES

- Leadership
- Ownership
- Integrity
- Passion for Winning
- Trust

PRINCIPLES

- We show respect for all individuals.
- The interests of the company and the individual are inseparable.
- We are strategically focused in our work.
- Innovation is the cornerstone of our success.
- We are externally focused. [customer focused]
- We value personal mastery. [professional expertise]
- We seek to be the best.
- Mutual interdependency is a way of life.

Renters v. Owners

We usually think of a renter as someone who pays a monthly fee to occupy property owned by someone else. The terms "renter" and "owner" can also apply to the mentality employees or volunteers bring to any organization. Below is a comparison.

Renters—Nothing against renters, but their contribution to any organization is confined to a low ceiling of self-interest. Their best efforts are prompted by external rewards like retaining a job, gaining recognition, increasing compensation, or securing a promotion. Renters stay engaged as long as they perceive their interests are served and that they are being adequately rewarded for their work. Whatever their motivation, good renters do as they are told and act primarily within the framework of their job description—but not much more. It is a rare renter who will give extra effort to upgrade the property or position of the organization they temporarily occupy.

Owners—Owners have a decidedly different perspective from renters. Ownership is not a set of formal obligations associated with a position. Ownership is a mindset, a set of beliefs about the work that overflows into attitudes and concrete actions. Owners want to be part of something greater than the immediate task or their job descriptions. Owners decide, act, and relate in ways that advance the goals of the organization, both within and beyond their job description. Owners possess a simple confidence that difficulties must be overcome, important work accomplished, and that it is up to them to make it happen. Owners take risks.

Whether you own or rent does make a difference. Owners stay for the long haul. Renters are just passing through. Owners embody the place. Renters sample the place. Owners invest. Renters withdraw. Owners are producers. Renters are consumers. Owners play the game. Renters watch. Owners are deeply connected. Renters glide and slide along the surface of organization life.

Owners have a clear mutual interest, not just a common philosophy. They have a stake to protect. Corporations often expect employees to think and act like owners but fail to give them a stake, including responsibility and authority.

A CLASSIC COMPARISON

I (Mark) visited the old Soviet Union in the late 1980s. On a bright, warm Saturday morning in May, I walked through a vast neighborhood of apartment complexes in suburban Moscow. As I took in the sights and sounds of the morning, a single impression came to mind—this neighborhood was quiet, motionless.

Back home on the previous Saturday, I had been awakened at 7:00 a.m. by the sound of a neighbor's power saw. Moments later another neighbor began unloading landscape rock in his driveway. Soon, another neighbor fired up his lawn mower.

But this Moscow neighborhood was dead quiet at 10:00 a.m. Then it struck me. No one in this vast collection of gritty, dreary apartment buildings had anything to take care of, to improve, or to upgrade. Under the Communist system, the average citizen could not own property. The Soviet Union was literally a nation of renters. And this rental neighborhood, like thousands across the country, bore silent testimony to the truth that renters are not concerned with fixing up, taking care of, or otherwise investing in what they do not own.

2

The 4-R Model of Transformational Leadership

The Ancient Text— The Book of Nehemiah 2:1-10

Nehemiah Goes to Jerusalem

¹Early the following spring, in the month of Nisan, during the twentieth year of King Artaxerxes' reign, I was serving the king his wine. I had never before appeared sad in his presence. ² So the king asked me, "Why are you looking so sad? You don't look sick to me. You must be deeply troubled."

Then I was terrified, ³ but I replied, "Long live the king! How can I not be sad? For the city where my ancestors are buried is in ruins, and the gates have been destroyed by fire."

⁴ The king asked, "Well, how can I help you?"

With a prayer to the God of heaven, ⁵ I replied, "If it please the king, and if you are pleased with me, your servant, send me to Judah to rebuild the city where my ancestors are buried."

⁶ The king, with the queen sitting beside him, asked, "How long will you be gone? When will you return?" After I told him how long I would be gone, the king agreed to my request.

⁷ I also said to the king, "If it please the king, let me have letters addressed to the governors of the province west of the Euphrates River, instructing them to let me travel safely through their territories on my way to Judah. ⁸ And please give me a letter addressed to Asaph, the manager of the king's forest, instructing him to give me timber. I will need it to make beams for the gates of the Temple fortress, for the city walls, and for a house for myself." And the king granted these requests, because the gracious hand of God was on me.

⁹ When I came to the governors of the province west of the Euphrates River, I delivered the king's letters to them. The king, I should add, had sent along army officers and horsemen to protect me. ¹⁰ But when Sanballat the Horonite and Tobiah the Ammonite official heard of my arrival, they were very displeased that someone had come to help the people of Israel.

Nehemiah's Story Updated

Jotham could not believe his ears. His friend Nehemiah had actually spilled the beans to King Artaxerxes about his plan to restore the Jews' capital city. Admittedly, the cupbearer had picked a good time. A little lubricated and in a good mood, the king had his queen next to him, which meant he was in the official request granting mode. But to answer truthfully when Artaxerxes, the most powerful man in the world, asked why Nehemiah was sad— that took either a lot of guts or a lot of dumb. Nehemiah could have faked illness or slapped a silly grin on his face; instead, he dared to tell the king the truth—he was homesick.

What happened next was even more incredible. Instead of telling Nehemiah to cheer up and get over it, the King had actually asked Nehemiah what he wanted. Imagine royalty asking a servant what would make him happy. But Artaxerxes seemed to trust that whatever Nehemiah wanted would be good for him as well.

Jotham watched from the corner as his friend breathed a quick prayer, and then dropped his bombshell. "I want to travel to the city of my fathers and restore it," said Nehemiah. The cupbearer took a deep breath, knowing the magnitude and unprecedented nature of what he was about to ask. "And if it please the King, could he graciously grant the building materials for this project and authorize my safe passage to Jerusalem?" To Jotham's amazement, Artaxerxes agreed Nehemiah's requests and provided an armed escort for the eight hundred mile journey.

Poor Jotham. He was still puzzling over what he'd just seen when the king turned to him. "Court Reporter!" he said. "I want you to go with Nehemiah to Jerusalem, and bring back a full report of all that happens."

"Yes sir!" said Jotham, half frantic at what he imagined a suicide mission. At the same time, he was curious what he would witness. As a writer, this could be his big break.

"That's what I get for hanging around with a guy like Nehemiah," he said under his breath. "Big dreams…always with the big dreams." Yet Nehemiah's honesty and boldness impressed Jotham, who secretly longed to be part of something greater than his own petty self-interest—something life changing. Though fearful, he was almost glad to get out of this hothouse of politics and embark on an adventure that might mean a brighter future for his own people.

Then he remembered the tribes who had fiercely opposed the Jews last time they tried to rebuild the wall, and Jotham began quaking in his boots. "What about the dreaded Horonites and Ammonites?" he thought. "We'll be headed straight toward them." Strangely, Jotham was actually relieved to be going on this potentially dangerous mission with Nehemiah, whose integrity and personal presence seemed to have a calming effect on all those around him.

The reporter headed for his apartment to pack.

Overview of the 4-R Model

At the beginning of this book, we described two contemporary theories of leadership—transformational and transactional. In the Prologue, in Chapter 1, and in the beginning of Chapter 2 you have been introduced to the remarkable success story of a man named Nehemiah, who lived 2,500 years ago and who exhibited many characteristics true of today's most effective leaders. In coming chapters, we

Co-author Mark McCloskey devised the 4-R Model in the 1990s to illustrate transformational leadership.

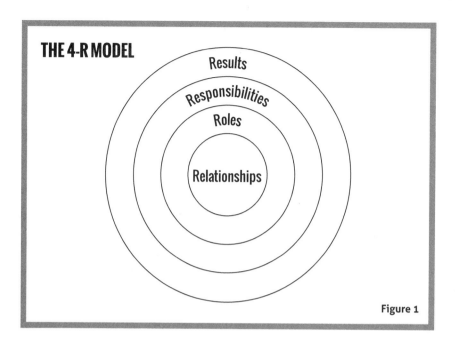

THE 4-R MODEL

Results

Responsibilities

Roles

Relationships

Figure 1

will explain in more detail how Nehemiah fit the mold of a transformational leader.

But first, we'll give you a bird's eye view of how the Theory of Transformational Leadership works. This is best accomplished by acquainting you with *The 4-R Model of Transformational Leadership*. Theories explain, while models exemplify. The 4-R Model is a graphic working model, sometimes called a pictorial representation, which illustrates the Theory of Transformational Leadership in action.

The 4-R Model assumes four critical factors come into play in any and all leadership situations: *Relationships*, *Roles*, *Responsibilities,* and *Results*. *See Figure 1.*

RELATIONSHIPS

The vast majority of leadership challenges and opportunities are relational in nature. So the first "R" of The 4-R Model stands for Relationships. At the core of the model, Relationships is the driving force of the effective transformational leader.

Of primary importance to this core are those capacities or "virtues" that allow the leader to relate to others in a transformational manner. These virtues are prudence (practical wisdom and humility), justice (fairness), fortitude (courage), temperance (moderation), faith, hope and love.

The 4-R Model folds all seven virtues into four traits of consequence, offering a helpful way to remember what is required to establish and maintain effective transformational Relationships. These traits are critical to any and all leadership situations, and the presence or absence of them is a reliable predictor of effective or poor leadership. Known by their acronym **DICE**, these traits of consequence are:

- **D**ynamic Determination

- **I**ntellectual Flexibility

- **C**ourageous Character

- **E**motional Maturity

Dynamic Determination—This trait is a cluster of attitudes and behaviors that draw upon the cardinal virtues of faith, hope, fortitude, and prudence. These virtues supply leaders with inner strength to initiate action in the face of obstacles, to avoid shrinking back in the face of resistance, and to sustain constructive activity in the face of adversity. Dynamic Determination links us to a larger purpose in life, generates the passion to live out that purpose, and gives wisdom to set daily priorities in light of that purpose.

> The word dynamic, in this context, refers to the kind of determination that listens to wisdom and makes necessary adjustments, as opposed to the kind of determination that acts like a bull in a china shop.

Intellectual Flexibility—Based on the cardinal virtue of prudence (practical wisdom and humility), Intellectual Flexibility refers to a leader's ability to see themselves, others, and the world clearly. This insight, coupled with the moral strength to change their attitudes and behavior in accordance with what is seen, allows transformational leaders to choose a wise course of action in the context of a larger purpose. Leaders with this trait determine what any given situation demands and act in light of that knowledge.

Courageous Character—Courageous Character is a cluster of attitudes and behaviors which draw on the cardinal virtues of love and fortitude (courage). This trait refers to a leader's moral integrity, which is the inner strength to live in accordance with high moral standards. Transformational leaders must carry a high level of moral courage and integrity to be trusted. Courageous Character is the strength to do the right thing when it's not the easy or popular thing to do—to stand strong for the people, organizations, and causes in their care. Courage and love are inseparable.

Emotional Maturity—This trait is a cluster of virtuous attitudes and behaviors which draw on the cardinal virtues of hope and temperance. Leaders with high emotional maturity stay solid when times are turbulent and the pressure is on; they don't flee, fight, or freeze. They remain connected with anxious and discouraged people and exercise a calming effect.

UNPACKING DICE + 1

Trait of Consequence	Virtues in this Trait	Characteristics
D DYNAMIC DETERMINATION	Faith, Hope, Fortitude, and Prudence	This trait links the leader to a larger purpose in life, generates the passion to live out that purpose, and gives wisdom to set daily priorities in light of that purpose.
I INTELLECTUAL FLEXIBILITY	Prudence (practical wisdom and humility)	Leaders with this trait determine what any given situation demands and act in light of that knowledge.
C COURAGEOUS CHARACTER	Love and Fortitude (courage)	Courageous Character gives a leader the strength to do the right thing when it's not the easy or popular thing to do.
E EMOTIONAL MATURITY	Hope and Temperance	Leaders with this trait stay solid when times are turbulent and and the pressure is on: they don't flee, fight, or freeze.
+1 COLLABORATIVE QUOTIENT	**Partner-up-ability**	**A leader with sufficient critical levels of DICE possesses the capacity to grow collaborative partnerships with a diverse array of people over time and across situations.**

Such leaders must have resolved basic issues of power, esteem and identity in order to deal with difficult situations and difficult people.

A leader with sufficient critical levels of **DICE** (Dynamic Determination, Intellectual Flexibility, Courageous Character and Emotional Maturity) possesses a key macro competency. *Collaborative Quotient* (or **+ 1**) is the summative expression of the leader's **DICE** configuration. It refers to her ability to initiate, sustain, and grow collaborative partnerships with a diverse array of people over time and across situations.

The higher a leader's **DICE + 1** capacity, the greater is that leader's capacity to play a variety of parts (see Roles below) and to sustain effective leadership activities (see Responsibilities below). The lower a leader's **DICE + 1** capacity, the smaller is that leader's capacity to collaborate. The effectiveness of a leader with low **DICE + 1** is greatly diminished.

ROLES

Transformational leadership is always a group endeavor, featuring leaders and followers (who are also leaders in their own smaller spheres) going to a better place. The next "R" in The 4-R Model stands for the Roles every leader must assume to lead their followers well over time.

This model identifies four macro Roles, each with its own unique set of obligations. *See Figure 2.* Pictured on a grid, each Role represents a corner of organizational life with an emphasis outside or inside the organization and a focus on today or tomorrow. The four Roles are:

- Direction Setter

- Spokesperson

- Coach

- Change Agent

Direction Setter (*Outside–Tomorrow*)—In the Direction Setter Role, the leader clarifies the larger purpose, unique mission, deep identity, and core values of the organization and infuses the organization with a philosophy of service. The mandate of the Direction Setter Role is to foster a cultural climate favorable to directional clarity and missional integrity, such that the organization lives in daily accord with its purpose, mission, identity, and core values.

Spokesperson *(Outside–Today)*—In this Role, the leader actively engages those the organization intends to serve—customers, shareholders, constituents, and others who are not part of the organization but on whose behalf the organization works. The leader as Spokesperson builds and sustains a customer-engaged culture, shaping the organization into an accessible and engaging place that regularly connects the people and resources of the organization with the needs and concerns of those outside the organization.

Coach *(Inside–Today)*—In the Coach Role, the leader places emphasis on the identification, development, and deployment of leaders to perpetuate and expand the work of the organization. The mandate of the Coach Role is to foster a leadership-friendly culture, which embraces new leaders and affords them opportunity to contribute to the welfare and progress of the organization.

Change Agent *(Inside–Tomorrow)*—The leader as Change Agent prompts and supports a continuous, collective focus on constructive change

> The Roles grid presented here draws from the work of University of Southern California Professor of Management Bert Nanus in his 1992 book, *Visionary Leadership*.

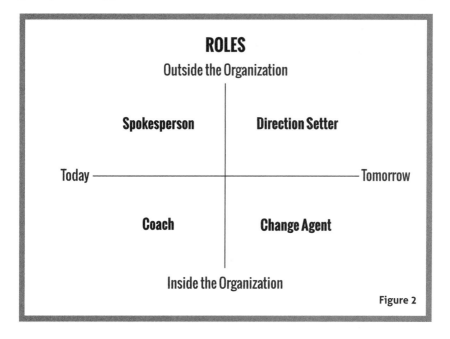

ROLES

Outside the Organization

Spokesperson Direction Setter

Today —————————————— Tomorrow

Coach Change Agent

Inside the Organization

Figure 2

and an emphasis on learning, in accordance with the purpose, mission, identity, and core values of the organization. The mandate of the Change Agent Role is to foster a cultural climate conducive to innovation and learning. Such a climate promotes changes in personal and organizational habits, attitudes, and practices that maintain the organization's effectiveness in a changing and unpredictable world.

The above Roles are not limited to a few gifted people at the top. For instance, the role of Direction Setter is not about the leader unilaterally defining the purpose, mission, vision, and strategic intent of the organization. Defining purpose is a collaborative endeavor where leaders with sufficiently high **DICE + 1** engage followers in candid, important discussions around the direction of the organization and its strategic priorities. Collaboration precludes the leader unilaterally imposing her sense of direction on the organization with no input from followers.

The same is true with all Roles and Responsibilities.

RESPONSIBILITIES

The third "R" in The 4-R Model stands for Responsibilities. Responsibilities depict the four activities in which all transformational leaders must participate. Like Relationships and Roles, the Responsibilities category is not a catchall list of every important activity that some leaders might do. Rather, it pictures the essential activities every leader must do to lead well over time in each of the Roles. *See Figure 3.* The four responsibilities are:

- Vision Casting

- Strategy Making

- Aligning

- Encouraging

Vision-Casting—This is the process by which the transformational leader and his followers craft, communicate, and continually revise an intellectually credible and emotionally engaging picture of a preferable future for an organization. Vision generates momentum, attracts and inspires individuals, and engages the entire organization in a collective effort to achieve

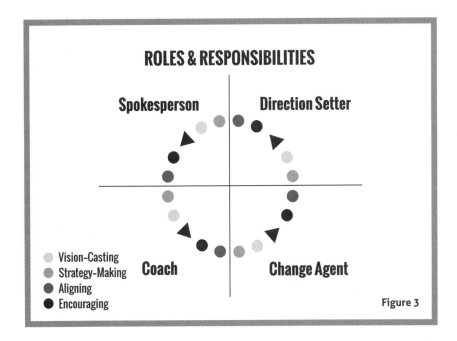

ROLES & RESPONSIBILITIES

Spokesperson   Direction Setter

○ Vision-Casting
◐ Strategy-Making   Coach   Change Agent
● Aligning
● Encouraging   Figure 3

higher purpose. Here again, Vision-Casting is a group effort, not reserved for a few gifted people at the top. The leader functions as a catalyst for collaboration so that many can participate in planning a bright future.

Strategy-Making—If we define leadership as helping a group of people get from Point A to Point B, Strategy-Making is creating a road map for the journey. This activity provides the first level of detail as to how the vision will be worked out in the day-to-day of the real world. In the work of Strategy-Making, the leader collaborates with her followers to create a coherent and integrated conceptual framework—a pattern of collective effort necessary to realize the vision.

Aligning—Aligning refers to the work of fostering commitment to the organization and its mission, and finding practical ways for followers to make valued contributions within the framework of the strategies agreed upon. The leader is responsible for bringing the hearts and minds of the followers—and with it their attention, talent, and resources—to the work of implementing the vision by creating a deep sense of ownership. The simplest way to explain aligning is the process of transforming renters into owners. *See Renters v. Owners on page 32.*

Encouraging—Encouraging is about imparting courage and hope to

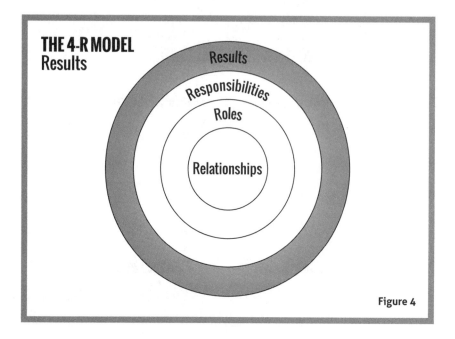

THE 4-R MODEL
Results

Results

Responsibilities

Roles

Relationships

Figure 4

others. A transformational leader infuses his followers with hope, instills a spirit of optimistic resolution, and sustains their morale and energy, especially in difficult times. This practice of inspirational communication, which is radically different from conventional motivation, results in greater emotional attachment to the cause (ownership), confidence that what a follower is doing is making a difference, and the willingness to collaborate with others to solve or prevent workplace problems.

RESULTS

Results make up the outer ring of The 4-R Model. This fourth "R" pictures the hard reality that organizations count on leaders to get things done. Results are the outcomes that flow from the implementation of Responsibilities in the context of a leader's Roles, as initiated and sustained by her Relationships. *See Figure 4.*

In the logic of the model, when a **DICE + 1** leader plays all four Roles and collaborates with followers in the four Responsibilities, then Results should follow.

In reality, there is rarely a 1:1 correlation between input and Results in the messy process of transformation. The future rarely arrives on time.

Rather, it comes in bits and pieces and fits and starts. Along the way, transformational leaders and their followers must monitor progress and make adjustments in the investment of time, energy, and resources, while keeping the purpose, mission, vision, and values of the organization in view.

There you have it—a summary of The 4-R Model. In coming chapters, we'll provide more detailed explanations and examples of how the Relationships, Roles, Responsibilities, and Results of transformational leaders and their followers work together to produce a better future for all—a future which more fully embodies their personal and collective vision and honors their shared values.

Before that, we'll address one question you may already be asking.

Why a Virtue-Based Model?

Transformational leadership is a relational and social endeavor requiring unique traits and behaviors to bring about deep and lasting change in times like these when broken dreams and hopelessness are common.

Some models emphasize traits of temperament (cognitive and emotional qualities) which may be helpful to a leader in influencing, directing, and motivating followers. While we acknowledge the significance of natural attributes like mental prowess, charisma, and even physical stamina, The 4-R Model places primary emphasis on the virtue of a leader.

We consider the leader's moral character of greatest importance to a process of transformation that is driven by the vision and values of all involved. As such, the success of a transformational leader will ultimately and necessarily be based on his or her virtue. Often defined as moral excellence, the English word virtue (from which we derive the words virile and virtuoso) comes from the Latin "virtus" meaning strength. In The 4-R Model of Transformational Leadership, *virtue is moral strength placed in service of others*.

There is a strong theoretical basis for including virtue as a first step to effective transformational leadership. Transformational leadership is an inherently moral undertaking focused on securing what both leaders and followers agree is good and right. Transformational leaders display a strong conviction in the moral rightness of their beliefs, adhere to high ethical standards, and live out those standards.

The question then becomes, "What standards or virtues are non-negotiable in the character of an effective transformational leader?" The Greeks, most notably Plato and Aristotle, created much of our vocabulary of virtue. They embraced prudence (practical wisdom and humility), justice (fairness), fortitude (courage) and temperance (moderation) as the moral glue that holds communities together.

The other great source of virtue language is Judeo-Christian, especially the virtues of faith, hope and love emphasized by St. Paul. St. Thomas Aquinas integrated these virtues with the Greek virtues and called them cardinal virtues from the Latin "cardo." Cardo means anything of fundamental or basic importance—a hinge or fixed point on which all other virtues turn. These seven cardinal virtues—prudence, justice, fortitiude, temperance, faith, hope and love—have proven their worth throughout history.

To demonstrate how these virtues play out in the life of a transformational leader, The 4-R Model folds them into four traits of consequence: Dynamic Determination, Intellectual Flexibility, Courageous Character and Emotional Maturity or **DICE**. These traits and the virtues they represent are surprisingly few. Even more surprising is how few people manifest these capacities. Unlike natural traits bestowed on us at birth, however, these traits of consequence may be learned. *See Virtue Can Be Learned on page 133.*

William Wilberforce: A Virtue-Based Leader

We greatly admire individuals who persevere in the midst of adversity, and well we should. It's practically impossible to accomplish anything of lasting worth without staying the course. Perseverance is the outworking of two cardinal virtues—prudence (practical wisdom and humility) and fortitude (courage).

History provides us with shining examples of men and women who took the initiative to act, persevered in the face of overwhelming obstacles, and finished what they started. One such example is social reformer William Wilberforce.

British-born Wilberforce (1759-1833) packed a lot of living into his more than seventy-three years—most notably leading the charge over four decades for the abolition of the slave trade in the British Empire.

The Setting—Between 1700 and 1810, British merchants transported almost three million Africans across the Atlantic to work in British-owned plantations in the West Indies. Appalling conditions aboard the slave ships killed many before they arrived, and some committed suicide on the journey.

To the average British citizen, however, slavery was a hidden scandal. Since human trafficking was prohibited inside Great Britain after 1772, its toll in human misery remained comfortably out of sight.

Besides, slavery was one of Great Britain's most profitable industries. Slave-grown produce accounted for 80 percent of that country's foreign income. Owners of the slave plantations would return to Great Britain and use their profits to purchase vast estates, as well as seats in Parliament. So slavery had become firmly embedded in the British economic and political system.

Enter the Reformer—William Wilberforce was an unlikely man to take on the vested interests of the most powerful nation on earth. He stood only five feet tall and by all accounts was homely and physically frail. What's more, his attentions were otherwise occupied. As a young university student, Wilberforce devoted himself to a lifestyle of partying and gambling at the elite social clubs of London.

But he was a dynamic speaker with a keen mind and great powers of persuasion, and in 1780, he won a prestigious seat in Parliament that guaranteed him a bright future.

The Change—In 1784-85, Wilberforce went through a reflective, spiritual process resulting in his conversion to Christianity. His spiritual transformation radically altered the trajectory of his life. He gave up drinking and gambling and resigned from his social clubs. His faith informed his politics, and in 1787 Wilberforce lent his legislative position and considerable persuasive powers to right a terrible wrong. He became a national leader in the anti-slave trade movement.

The Race—At first, Wilberforce naively assumed the forces

aligned with the slave-trade would see the wrong of their ways, relent, and grant the cause a quick victory. He was mistaken. His foes fought back vigorously. Wilberforce was physically assaulted twice, challenged to a duel, and threatened with death numerous times. For two years, a discredited slave trader stalked Wilberforce, forcing him to travel with an armed body guard. In addition, he endured years of public ridicule from Great Britain's most powerful people, including the king. Wilberforce became the empire's most vilified man.

Throughout the decade of the 1790s, Wilberforce introduced abolition bills in Parliament, but to no avail. The pattern of rejections continued year after year as legislation was defeated by stiff resistance from the West India interests. War with France and waning enthusiasm among the British public caused many abolitionists to lose heart entirely and withdraw from the campaign. Wilberforce did not.

Instead, he marshaled those against the slave-trade to engage in a new strategy of public, mass petitioning to exert pressure on Parliament to abolish the slave trade. That strategy almost worked; the House of Lords resolved to gradually abolish the trade, but the House of Commons refused to revive the subject—effectively killing the legislation.

In his later years, the stress and strain of the quest to abolish slavery took a physical and emotional toll on Wilberforce but, encouraged by others, he persisted. Finally, after twenty years of rejection, his legislation banning the purchase, sale, and transport of slaves was adopted in 1807. With half the battle won, Wilberforce and his allies worked tirelessly over the next twenty-six years to abolish slavery throughout the British Empire.

The Finish Line—In his sixties and in failing health, Wilberforce was regarded throughout the world as one of the greatest men of his generation. An Italian diplomat remarked on viewing the opening of Parliament that "everyone contemplates this little old man, worn with age, and a head sunk in his shoulders...as the Washington of humanity."

Three days before Wilberforce died in 1883, the House of Commons passed the Abolition of Slavery bill and the following year over eight hundred thousand slaves throughout the British Empire were set free.

The Importance of Virtue—William Wilberforce could not have predicted the implacable opposition that would arise when his cause of abolishing slavery jeopardized the economic interests of the nation. Nor could he have known it would take over twenty years to abolish the slave trade and another twenty-six years to emancipate existing slaves. Nevertheless he persisted and has become to us today a shining example of a person who accomplished extraordinary things against insurmountable odds.

Wilberforce and his allies succeeded because his leadership was based on the virtues of faith, hope, fortitude, and prudence which he adopted early in his adult life. These virtues gave him inner strength to initiate action in the face of obstacles, to avoid shrinking back in the face of resistance, and to persevere in the face of adversity (Dynamic Determination). Wilberforce also maintained a clear view of his world and the flexibility to change strategies, as he saw the need, to better position his cause for success (Intellectual Flexibility). His high level of moral strength to do the right thing when it was not easy or popular attracted more and more supporters, resulting in the eventual abolition of slavery (Courageous Character). Moreover, his freedom from the need to be popular or to accumulate power allowed him to focus on the task throughout years of opposition and to encourage others who, in turn, encouraged him in the darkest of times (Emotional Maturity).

Based on seven cardinal virtues, the **DICE** traits of Dynamic Determination, Intellectual Flexibility, Courageous Character and Emotional Maturity shone brightly in the life of William Wilberforce. These traits gave him the wherewithal to initiate, grow, and sustain collaborative partnershipswith a diverse array of people. That's **DICE + 1**. Over time, Wilberforce and his allies accomplished substantial and lasting good for millions of his countrymen. That's what real transformational leadership looks like.

GAINING PERSONAL PERSPECTIVE

Like Jotham, have you ever longed to be part of something greater than your own self-interests?

_____

Which of the seven cardinal virtues do you bring to the task of leadership? If virtue is teachable, which would you like to learn?

_____

_____

_____

_____

The loftiness of William Wilberforce's goal to end slavery appears to have trumped power, prestige and personal ambition early in his political life. What goal is so compelling that you are willing to give up personal gains to achieve it?

_____

_____

_____

_____

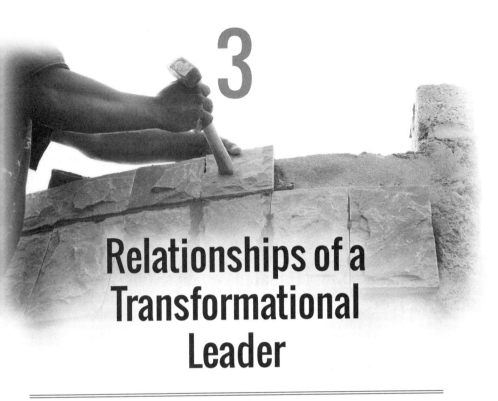

Relationships of a Transformational Leader

The Ancient Text— The Book of Nehemiah 2:11-20

Nehemiah Inspects Jerusalem's Wall

^{11} So I arrived in Jerusalem. Three days later, ^{12} I slipped out during the night, taking only a few others with me. I had not told anyone about the plans God had put in my heart for Jerusalem. We took no pack animals with us except the donkey I was riding. ^{13} After dark I went out through the Valley Gate, past the Jackal's Well, and over to the Dung Gate to inspect the broken walls and burned gates. ^{14} Then I went to the Fountain Gate and to the King's Pool, but my donkey couldn't get through the rubble. ^{15} So, though it was still dark, I went up the Kidron Valley instead, inspecting the wall before I turned back and entered again at the Valley Gate.

^{16} The city officials did not know I had been out there or what I was doing, for I had not yet said anything to anyone about my plans. I had not yet spoken to the Jewish leaders—the priests, the nobles, the officials, or anyone else in the administration. ^{17} But now I said to them, "You know very well what trouble we are in. Jerusalem lies in ruins, and its gates have been destroyed by fire. Let us rebuild the wall of Jerusalem and end this disgrace!" ^{18} Then I told them about how the gracious *hand of God had been on me, and about my conversation with the king.*

They replied at once, "Yes, let's rebuild the wall!" So they began the good work.

[19] But when Sanballat, Tobiah, and Geshem the Arab heard of our plan, they scoffed contemptuously. "What are you doing? Are you rebelling against the king?" they asked.

[20] I replied, "The God of heaven will help us succeed. We, his servants, will start rebuilding this wall. But you have no share, legal right, or historic claim in Jerusalem."

Nehemiah's Story Updated

It was a long, dusty 900 miles by camel to Jerusalem, with many dangers along the way. Jotham was ecstatic to finally see the broken-down walls of the ancient city come into view and to slip down off his beast for the very last time. What a relief that Nehemiah decided to rest a few days before conducting any official business that required Jotham's report.

Then one night Nehemiah roused the Court Reporter out of a sound sleep. "Get up, Jotham," whispered his friend. "We're going to do a little reconnaissance." Accompanied by two trusted aides who had traveled with them to Jerusalem, the duo left Jerusalem by one of the few recognizable gates in the ruined south wall. They made their way without torches, relying on a full moon to light their way. No one saw them leave.

Threading their way through the ruins of the old wall was tricky. Nehemiah, the only one on a mule, led the procession, and it was a good thing. The sure-footed animal's keen eyes and ears helped them avoid gaps in the rubble too tight to fit through. In the end, the men surveyed just a fraction of the ruined wall before returning to the city. But their survey must have been enough to give Nehemiah a plan. Two days later, Nehemiah called the city leaders together. *"What would he say?"* thought Jotham, well aware that some of these men had profitable relationships with neighboring tribes precisely because Jerusalem had no walls.

Nehemiah began by rehearsing the problem that had persisted for 142 years–broken down defenses, a community in disgrace, and the dishonor this brought to the God they worshiped. Next, the newly arrived governor laid out the vision that God had given him months before to rebuild their community, beginning with the walls. He described the day he presented this request to King Artaxerxes, and how the king not only approved but also agreed to supply wood for Jerusalem's gates. Jotham watched faces in the crowd turn from skepticism to awe as they realized this was the same king who had fourteen years before put a stop to their construction.

Nehemiah brushed aside the opportunity to flex his muscles as their newly appointed governor but instead appealed to their shared values as children of Israel. The broken walls weren't only Nehemiah's problem, nor would the vision of a single human being solve this decades-long predicament. The need to rebuild their security and community was everyone's problem, and they would share equally in the solution. Nehemiah used terms like "we" and "us" liberally as he appealed for work to begin on the wall. When he finished, the city leaders replied in unison, "We're with you—bring it on!"

Bad and good news travels fast. Predictably the local tribes, who had controlled the economy of Jerusalem and the surrounding countryside, accused Nehemiah and the city's leaders of treason. Jotham expected his friend to cut the tribes a deal or to flaunt the Jews' new political status with Artaxerxes, but Nehemiah amazed the court reporter by appealing to an even higher authority, and basically telling the squatters to get lost.

Now Jotham had his big story. Talk about front page news.

Virtue-Based Relationships: Core of the 4-R Model

Effective leadership flows from the heart. Ultimately the leader's exercise of virtue—a matter of the heart—is the critical factor in his or her success. The heart of our ancient friend Nehemiah, for instance, was connected to God's purposes for the people of Israel. Wherever and whenever sustained transformation occurs, results come less from the leadership skills of a man or a woman, however helpful they may be, and more from what is in the heart of that leader. That is why we've positioned virtue-based relationships at the center of The 4-R Model. *See Figure 5.*

Now it is entirely possible for an individual to exhibit a virtue or characteristic of moral excellence in isolation. For instance, she may well be

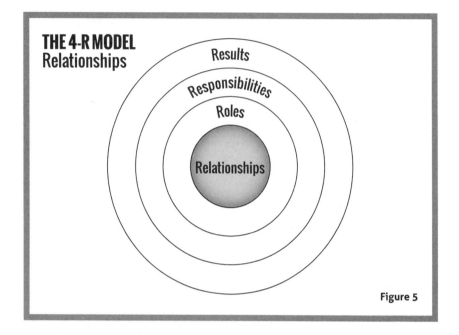

THE 4-R MODEL
Relationships

Results

Responsibilities

Roles

Relationships

Figure 5

dedicated to a purpose higher than her own self-interest. But as soon as that person takes that characteristic into the leadership arena, it becomes relational. Leadership is by definition a social phenomenon. The ancient Greeks and the early Christians never viewed virtue as distinct from community life and interpersonal relationships. As a result, The 4-R Model—with virtue-based relationships at its core—assumes that truly transformative leadership happens in the context of a community or an organization.

LEADERSHIP FROM THE INSIDE OUT

Anyone aspiring to transformational leadership must:

- Commit to a purpose larger than oneself.

- Develop virtue—the **DICE + 1** traits of consequence.

- Effectively collaborate with others.

First, she must commit to a purpose larger than herself. This commitment may assume various forms. It may be devotion to God, or it could be the conviction that each human being must be concerned for the welfare of the whole or for the least among us. International speaker and leadership consultant Henry Cloud calls this commitment "transcendence" and defines it as living for a higher, nobler purpose than one's self.

The default, of course, is to live a very small life, focused around one's own self- interest, as exemplified by the character Gordon Gekko played by Michael Douglas in the 1987 20th Century Fox film *Wall Street*. A notorious corporate raider, Gekko lectures shareholders of a company he has taken over, summarizing his philosophy in one audacious sentence, "Greed, for lack of a better word, is good."

> True transformation happens not because of leadership skill but because of what is in a leader's heart.

The Virtue-Leadership Connection

It's fair to ask, "Why are virtue-based Relationships (introduced in Chapter 2) so central to transformational leadership?" The simple answer is that there is a direct correlation between a leader's effectiveness and the virtues possessed by that leader.

All leadership Responsibilities talked about in Chapter 2 like Vision-Casting, Strategy-Making, Aligning and Encouraging followers to work toward a goal are ultimately dependent not just on the leader's skills but on the leader's virtue to undergird and sustain behaviors.

So wherever you find a leader successfully casting vision, you'll likely find a person who is locked into a larger purpose—that's the virtue-based trait of Dynamic Determination (also introduced in Chapter 2). Wherever you find a leader staying in touch with the external operating environment and formulating successful strategies, you'll likely find someone exercising the virtues of prudence, practical wisdom, and humility which make up Intellectual Flexibility. These are the first two traits of consequence critical to any and all transformational leadership situations. The other two are Courageous Character and Emotional Maturity.

We've chosen the acronym **DICE** as a simple and effective way of organizing and remembering these traits of consequence. All four **DICE** traits will be discussed in detail, later in this chapter.

This is a fairly common path which I (Jim) witnessed recently while waiting for a plane at the Dallas-Fort Worth International Airport. I overheard another businessman's cell phone conversation with a friend. He boasted about how he was going to leverage his relationships with a company to profit himself. He kept using phrases like "I am going to win" and "this will be incredibly profitable" and "my ship will come in." This eavesdropped conversation exemplifies one of two levels on which a transactional (*v.* transformational) leader can operate. It's the darker side of a zero-sum game where I win and you lose.

There is a somewhat brighter side to transactional leadership. This outcome was advocated by leadership guru Stephen R. Covey in his book *Seven Habits of Highly Effective People.* Covey urged a "win-win" strategy whereby you get what you want and I get what I want. But win-win is often only a way to ensure that I win. Again, we're faced with a low ceiling of self-interest when pursuing that form of leadership.

Nehemiah, on the other hand, entered his leadership role in the rebuilding of Jerusalem not with a win-win or win-lose strategy, but with a sense of service to a higher purpose at all costs—even if he lost. Transformational leaders put it all on the line, not knowing what will happen. Their lives are often full of ambiguity, lack of closure, and uncertainty—as we learned from the story of William Wilberforce in Chapter 2. But genuinely transformational leaders give everything anyway, because of their uncompromising commitment to a higher purpose.

Next, an aspiring leader must develop virtue. He must have settled internally certain character issues and possess the **DICE** traits of consequence that allow him to pursue a higher purpose and to relate to others effectively.

Finally, a leader who would be transformational must effectively manage her relationships with others. We refer to this as her Collaborative Quotient or **+ 1** capacity. Simply stated, this is a leader's ability to partner with followers espousing similar interests to create healthy, effective change in any organization. Consider the following examples of women who demonstrated these traits in generous measure.

Edith Stein: The Courageous Carmelite

Born into a Jewish family in Germany in 1891, Edith Stein possessed an extraordinary intellect and excelled at every academic level. A life-changing experience drew her to the question of faith and religion. Her journey led her to become a Carmelite nun and challenge the Pope's inaction over the Nazi persecution of the Jews. Despite her strong faith and dedication, she eventually perished in a concentration camp in 1942.

There are three instances where Stein demonstrated her capacity as a transformational leader: requesting a private audience with the Pope, the 1938 German elections, and declining safe asylum in Switzerland.

In 1933, Stein wrote to Pope Pius XI regarding her growing concern over the treatment of the Jews. Though in the minority, she followed her conviction and reached out to the pope "requesting a private audience during which to plead for an encyclical condemning Nazi anti-Semitism," says author James Carroll.

This act demonstrated a concern not only for her heritage, but for the entire Jewish population. Her ability to recognize a legitimate threat and swift action to work with a potential change agent in the Pope speaks volumes to her leadership. Though she could have avoided risk by hiding in her new faith, she proactively took issue with the conditions and advocated for action.

In 1938, Hitler was already in position to overtake and dominate the European continent. "The principles of National Socialism and the Government of Hitler had so clearly proved hostile to Christ and God that even the most unsuspecting German could no longer be in doubt about the goal at which they were aiming," said Robert Royal in *The Catholic Martyrs of the Twentieth Century*. This was especially vexing for the Cologne Carmelite forced to choose between voting for Hitler and suffering the consequences.

Stein discovered that her sisters at the convent planned to cast their votes in favor of Hitler to avoid further persecution. However, "she [Edith] vehemently opposed this infidelity to the truth, even for the best of motives, whatever the consequences," said Royal.

By standing for truth, Stein again disregarded her own safety and acted according to her belief, demonstrating her strong character by doing the right thing even though it might cost her.

The last event occurred when she declined relocation to Switzerland, a country known for its neutrality, making it a likely safe-haven from persecution. By this time, Stein's sister Rosa had converted to Catholicism and joined her sister at the convent in Holland. However, Hitler had already begun his invasion of Holland, and it was clear that no Jews would be safe. When the invasion began, Stein "sought asylum for herself and Rosa in the convent... in Switzerland...tragically, though the Swiss convent had room for Edith, it was already too crowded to take Rosa," continues Royal. Instead of seeking safety and self-preservation, Stein made the choice to not abandon her sister, which eventually led to her imprisonment and death.

Edith Stein is an exemplar of transformational leadership. She showed Dynamic Determination, Courageous Character and Emotional Maturity as she confronted the Nazis over their treatment of the Jews. She acted out of a deep sense of virtue—strength for others—by continually putting others first and fighting for what was right despite the consequences.

Harriet Tubman: Freedom Fighter

Harriet Tubman (1822-1913) was a giant in American history. She overcame social and political barriers to effect lasting change.

Born a slave on Maryland's eastern shore, Tubman is best known for her work as a conductor on the Underground Railroad, a lifeline for runaway slaves as they escaped to the North and Canada before and during the Civil War. Over an eight-year period she embodied the sense of higher purpose, passion, and perseverance found in Dynamic Determination as she led more than 300 slaves, including family and friends, to freedom. In her words, "I never ran my train off the track, and I never lost a passenger."

Tubman is an unparalleled example of the transforming power of Courageous Character as she repeatedly put her own freedom and safety at risk to secure the freedom of runaway slaves. Slaveholders placed a reward for her capture and the Fugitive Slave Act of 1850 imposed severe punishments on those who helped slaves escape. Upon hearing that her niece and her daughters were to be sold, she ventured back to Maryland and led her family members north.

Tubman's courage extended to the Civil War battlefield. In July of 1863, Tubman led Union troops under the command of Colonel James Montgomery in the Combahee River expedition. The mission was to disrupt Southern supply lines by destroying bridges and railroads. In the course of the campaign, more than 750 slaves were freed. In the words of General Rufus Saxton, who reported the raid to Secretary of War Stanton, "This is the only military command in American history wherein a woman, black or white, led the raid and under whose inspiration it was originated and conducted."

Tubman's long life of dedicated service defies categorization. To abolitionist John Brown, leader of the Harper's Ferry slave uprising, she was "General Tubman." To the slaves she led north, she was "Moses." To all, she was a prophetic voice for social justice, working for the cause of women's suffrage, and establishing schools for freed slaves in South Carolina. Whatever role Tubman played, she demonstrated the transforming power of Dynamic Determination and Courageous Character.

Ellen Johnson Sirleaf: Africa's Iron Lady

Ellen Johnson Sirleaf is a present-day example of Dynamic Determination and Courageous Character. Raised in the capital of Liberia, Sirleaf found herself excluded from privilege and opportunity because of her heritage. Yet she was determined to pursue a life beyond the limited prospects available to most West African women.

Sirleaf's resolve, combined with an interest in finance, led to her acceptance for study abroad. Eventually, she earned degrees in accounting, economics, and public administration—the latter from Harvard University's Kennedy School of Government.

She held prestigious posts within the World Bank and the United Nations. But she kept coming back to her native Liberia, despite personal risk and ridicule, trying to lead it to a better future. She ran for the Liberian Senate in 1985 and spent time in prison for her outspokenness. She ran for the presidency in 1997, and finished second in a field of thirteen candidates. Knowing the treacherous ways of her opponent, she entered self-imposed exile until his removal from office in 2003.

Sirleaf came back again and again as a champion against government corruption and the brutal suppression of opposing political viewpoints.

Finally, in 2005, Ellen Johnson Sirleaf succeeded in attaining Liberia's highest office. As Liberia's twenty-fourth president, Sirleaf became the first female head of state on the continent of Africa. In 2011, her fellow Liberians elected her to a second term, and that same year Africa's Iron Lady (as she is known internationally) received a Nobel Peace Prize for her non-violent struggle for peace and women's rights.

Ellen Johnson Sirleaf's story is one of Courageous Character. She took a stand against the corrupt and ruthless leadership, despite imprisonment, exile, and other deprivations. She relentlessly fought for what she believed, showing Dynamic Determination in her resolve to transform Liberia's political and social landscape. A woman in a male culture running against forty-eight other candidates for president in 2005, Ellen Johnson Sirleaf faced daunting odds. But her professional will, passion, and persistence enabled her to achieve her purpose.

In the end there are three directions an aspiring leader must look: UP to a purpose larger than one's self, INSIDE for the virtue to strive for that higher purpose, and OUT for the ability to partner with others to achieve that purpose.

If aspiring leaders do not serve a purpose larger than themselves, then their virtuous traits will not be as strong. If they are missing one or more of the **DICE** traits of consequence, then their **+1** ability to collaborate with others will suffer.

DICE+1 of a Transformational Leader

Assuming a relationship or a purpose larger than one's self, how does **DICE + 1** work in the life of a transformational leader? Let's take a closer look at these traits of consequence as they have been exhibited in the life of our ancient example, Nehemiah. Then, we'll consider more recent examples of transformational leaders and organizations.

We've already defined the "D" of **DICE + 1**, Dynamic Determination, as a combination of virtues which supply the leader with inner strength to initiate action in the face of obstacles, to avoid shrinking back in the face of resistance, and to sustain constructive activity in the face of adversity. The leader with Dynamic Determination is linked to a bigger purpose in life, giving him passion to live out the purpose and wisdom to set priorities that bring the purpose about.

Two thousand five hundred years ago, Nehemiah was very much focused on a purpose larger than his own self-interest. So much so that he traded a position of security, relative power, and influence for the opportunity to take on a challenge for which he had no personal responsibility or clear idea of the outcome. He did so because he believed his God had promised to return the Jews to their land and that he (Nehemiah) was in a position to help make that happen.

The Dynamic Determination exhibited by Nehemiah required a combination of faith, hope, fortitude, and prudence. He had faith in the purpose and provision of a being greater than himself. He had hope that a remedy to Jerusalem's insecurity and disgrace could be fashioned. He had fortitude to approach Artaxerxes with a request to support a project the king had personally forbidden fourteen years before. He had prudence to know how and when to approach all parties involved—the king, Jerusalem's leaders, and those opposed to rebuilding the wall.

Nehemiah also exhibited a high degree of Intellectual Flexibility, the

"I" of **DICE + 1**, which is the leader's ability to see the world clearly, coupled with the moral strength to change one's attitude and behavior in accordance with what is seen. This trait, which combines wisdom and humility, allows the leader to determine what any given situation demands and to choose a wise course of action.

Nehemiah was a man who read both the ancient writings of his people and the front pages of the daily newspaper. Part of his job, as the king's cupbearer, was to stay in touch with current events. He understood the desire of King Artaxerxes to repopulate areas of the empire like Judea that had been decimated by the Babylonians, as a catalyst to restarting their economies. This would be good for the whole of the Persian Empire which extracted an across-the-board 39 percent tax rate on all goods and services sold. Nehemiah also understood that Jerusalem's leaders had been rebuffed once before in their attempt to rebuild the walls, and that some might have reason not to support his plan for economic and social reasons. But Nehemiah surmised they would support the effort if he appealed to their common heritage and interest in seeing God's promises to the Jewish people fulfilled. He had Intellectual Flexibility.

Next, Nehemiah exhibited Courageous Character, the "C" of **DICE + 1**, from the time he decided to approach the king to the time he refused to compromise in any way with the enemy. He had resolved his core identity and refused to be two people. He was a Jew first and only then a cupbearer to the king or a governor in the Persian Empire. As such, it was not difficult for him to find the inner strength necessary to live in accordance with the high moral standards and integrity required by his God.

Some Jewish Leaders in 445 BC had profitable trading alliances and their children had intermarried with the tribes surrounding Jerusalem.

Nehemiah understood the pitfalls of teaming up with local idol-worshiping tribes. Rather than compromising, he cut them off entirely from involvement in the reconstruction effort or revitalization of the city. Judah's new governor truly showed he had the combined virtues of love and fortitude necessary to do the right thing when it was not the easy and popular thing to do.

Nehemiah exhibited Emotional Maturity the "E" of **DICE + 1**, both when he approached the king and when he stood firm in the face of opposition to the announcement of the wall rebuilding effort. As we will see in future chapters of this ancient writing, Nehemiah's emotional stability exerted a calming effect on workers rebuilding the wall. When opposition intensified, this newly arrived governor was able to quickly restore confidence and move the work forward.

Furthermore, Nehemiah had resolved any internal questions as to his need for control or recognition of his own power or status in the eyes of others. His love for the Jewish people and their homeland, his hope for their future, and his temperance is clearly seen in the way the new governor joined his interests with those of local leaders as he urged them to begin rebuilding the wall together. As a result, he was able to quickly align them with the project.

As we read in Chapters 1 and 2 of the ancient text, Nehemiah looked UP when he confessed wrongdoing on behalf of his people and prayed to God for intervention in their plight. In so doing, he appealed to a purpose larger than himself. Then, despite being very much afraid, he looked INSIDE for strength (generated by his faith and hope in God) to approach the king with a request for assistance, to encourage and align the leaders in Jerusalem, and to counter the opposition that immediately ensued. Finally, he looked OUTSIDE to others with similar interests to affect the changes needed to remedy the problem of the broken-down walls and the associated disgrace.

The final trait or macro-competency exhibited by Nehemiah was his capacity to initiate, sustain, and grow collaborative relationships with others of similar interests. The 4-R Model refers to this as Collaborative Quotient. Collaborative Quotient, also known as **+ 1**, is the cumulative expression of a leader's **DICE**. The higher a leader's **DICE + 1,** the greater is that leader's capacity to collaborate. Today, we would say Nehemiah had a high **DICE + 1** capacity. As a result, this former cupbearer was able to change a policy on rebuilding a wall that had stood for fourteen years. He was able to garner from the King's resources the timber needed for the project. He was also able to secure an official position as governor of Judea which gave him the authority to do what he had proposed, meriting an armed escort to assure the safe passage of his team to Jerusalem. Moreover, Nehemiah was able to win over the discouraged citizens of Jerusalem and align them with the task of building the wall, which would take virtually everyone away from their occupations for a period of fifty-two days. And he was able to rebuff local opposition to the project by area tribes.

Important: The **DICE** *traits of consequence tend to operate in unison. One rarely operates to the exclusion of the others. They come as a package and an effective transformational leader needs sufficient critical levels of all four—Dynamic Determination, Intellectual Flexibility, Courageous Character, and Emotional Maturity—to effectively Collaborate with others. If one trait of consequence is missing or below a sufficient critical level, it's like being on a deep body of water in a boat with a gash in the hull—catastrophic. A hole in a leader's* **DICE** *boat will diminish his ability to Collaborate and to assume the Roles and Responsibilities of a leader. A leader is transformational, not because of a name on a door or title but because of who she is. The good news is, these traits can be learned.*

Historic Examples of DICE

Human beings are designed to work best when linked to a purpose larger than their own self-interests. Studying historic individuals who lead in a transformational manner—like Nehemiah, William Wilberforce, and more recently Mother Theresa—we cannot help but conclude that people operate at their peak when they risk all for a noble cause. But can you and I identify with giants like these?

Though a member of a conquered people group, Nehemiah's occupation before rebuilding the walls of Jerusalem might be compared to today's secret service agent. He was close to the ultimate seat of power. William Wilberforce had an extraordinary command of the English language and the ability to sway the masses with his verbal skills. Mother Theresa has been placed on a pedestal so high the average person struggles to imagine herself influencing others in a similar manner. We may more readily identify with the likes of Joshua Chamberlain (profiled in Chapter 1) who excelled at academics but knew little about conducting a battle.

Abraham Lincoln's birth in a Kentucky log cabin may make him more accessible to us, although his assassination at the end of the Civil War has rendered our sixteenth president's image somewhat larger than life. Lincoln's passion for the survival of the Union and, later, for freeing the slaves, sustained him when it seemed all hope for both outcomes was lost (Dynamic Determination). At the beginning of his first term in office, he shrewdly formed a cabinet consisting largely of his political rivals which served him well during the early years of the Civil War (Intellectual Flexibility). Later, Lincoln refused to compromise the moral high ground of emancipation. Burning through much of the political capital earned during his first term, he pushed the Thirteenth Amendment through Congress before the Confederate surrender, thus assuring the abolition of slavery throughout the union (Courageous Character). The fact that he needed affirmation from no one nor a show of power to establish his credibility made it possible for Lincoln to find common ground with his critics and win them over during perhaps the most turbulent time in our nation's history (Emotional Maturity).

On the receiving end of the Thirteenth Amendment, Amanda Berry Smith also serves as a shining example of Emotional Maturity. Smith was born a slave in Maryland on January 23, 1837. Grinding poverty and paralyzing personal tragedy shaped her childhood and adult life. By the age of thirty, Smith had buried three of her children and two husbands. Like many black women of her generation, Smith assumed the role of a washerwoman—a life of unrelenting toil and drudgery.

In spite of crushing personal adversity, Smith distinguished herself as one of a handful of women who broke through ethnic and gender barriers to bridge the gulf between the races and the sexes at the end of the nineteenth century. She was an early advocate of women's suffrage, served as a national speaker for the Women's Christian Temperance Union, and as a charter member of the Illinois NAACP. She established the first orphanage in the world for black children.

The remarkable life of Amanda Berry Smith is a reminder that emotional strength comes not from without in the form of positive circumstances but from within in the form of one's emotional resources.

REAL UNKNOWN HEROES

Still, there may be some who claim these historic examples provide evidence for the Great Man Theory—that history has, in large part, unfolded as men and women of great intellect, charisma, and prowess across the global chessboard have made crucial and timely moves that changed the course of all humankind. These same would argue that leadership is born into, not learned. We disagree.

Hundreds of thousands of unsung heroes have lived, led transformationally, and died leaving this a better world. We may more readily connect with these individuals, both big **L** and little **l**, precisely because their stories have not been widely publicized. In her nineteenth century novel *Middlemarch*, Mary Anne Evans (under the pen name George Eliot) offers a sympathetic look at unknown and simple people living lives of quiet dignity and moral courage. She ends the book with these powerful words.

> *"For the growing good of the world is partly dependent on unhistoric acts; and that things are not so ill with you and me as they might have been, is half owing to the number who lived faithfully a hidden life, and rest in unvisited tombs."*

It would be difficult to find a better example of unheralded leaders than the Europeans who risked their lives to hide and help Jews in Nazi-occupied Europe during World War II. Dubbed the "rescuers," these ordinary people displayed moral and physical courage by sheltering Jews as Nazis tried to exterminate the race. The rescuers include a few famous examples like Swedish diplomat Raoul Wallenberg who may have saved as many as one hundred thousand Hungarian Jews, and German businessman Oskar Schindler whose list of employees essential to his industry protected up to 1,200 mostly Polish Jews from the gas chambers. But the majority of the rescuers escaped celebrity as they individually protected Jewish families or collaborated together—like the residents of an entire French mountain village, Le Chambon, who sheltered over five thousand Jews from the Nazis.

Years later, books written on the subject conclude that rescuers like the two families who hid Anne Frank risked their comfort, security, and very lives because it was the right thing to do. Many stubbornly refused to be called heroes because providing aid to those who needed it was simply the way they always treated other people before, during, and after the war.

Their actions were guided by an ethic, a purpose greater than themselves which gave them strength to participate in this great humanitarian mission while the vast majority of Europeans turned their backs. That's Dynamic Determination.

Furthermore, the rescuers possessed what could be termed deep personal integrity. They acted according to what they valued despite the fact that aiding Jews was a crime publishable by imprisonment, torture, or death. To turn away the Jewish family at their door would have been to turn away from who they knew themselves to be. That's Courageous Character.

Finally, these ordinary people aided and protected a vilified class of human beings despite the censure and disdain of neighbors and even family members who stood by and did nothing. They did not require the approval of others, only the approval of their own hearts. That's Emotional Maturity.

Jan Polanska, profiled in *When Light Pierced the Darkness*, saved ten Jews by hiding them in her small apartment. "I have to be at peace with myself," Polanska is quoted as saying. "What others think about me is not important. It is my own conscience that I must please and not the opinion of others."

WHEN VIRTUE IS ITS OWN REWARD

The example of the World War II rescuers banishes the notion that transformational leadership, based on virtue, is a strategy for success by the world's standards. It certainly has the potential to change things for the good, but virtue can also get a leader into trouble. Many who harbored Jews from the Nazis ended up in concentration camps or were executed. Two of the most well-known rescuers, Schindler and Wallenberg, experienced irrecoverable loss. Schindler spent his entire fortune protecting his employees and died penniless. Wallenberg was placed under arrest and died in a Russian gulag.

Risk, which infers both potential reward and possible failure, is inherent in the cardinal virtues of love and fortitude. These virtues combine to form the trait of consequence we call Courageous Character. Anyone who lives with moral integrity puts something at risk. Sometimes the risk pays off, but effective leaders follow a virtuous path even when the outcome is not guaranteed or known. Exhibiting Courageous Character may mean keeping one's integrity but losing one's job, friends, family, or even one's life. In that case, virtue must be its own reward.

Then again, living courageously may pay off, as it did for a man named Roy.

About 20 years ago, Roy and I (Mark) attended a Sunday School class together. He was an accountant and a talented young man. One Friday afternoon, Roy's boss approached him and asked him to do some "creative accounting". The man told Roy to cut a few corners, misreport a few items, and delay reporting some others. This violated Roy's sense of integrity. He came to our Sunday school class that weekend to ask his friends for advice. We concluded that Roy had two choices. He could either make the changes requested by his boss, or he could decline to make the changes, keep his integrity, and risk losing his job.

> **Effective leaders follow a virtuous path even when the outcome is not guaranteed.**

Roy decided on the latter option. He put it all on the line, refusing to make the changes his boss had requested. Next Sunday, Roy showed up and announced, "I'm unemployed." The previous Monday, his boss had fired him outright when he refused to engage in crooked accounting. By Tuesday, Roy had packed up all his things, had his ID taken from him, and was out of a job. But that's not the end of the story.

Two weeks later, Roy came back to class and told us, "The most amazing thing happened." His former boss had had lunch with a friend and told him the whole story. "You wouldn't believe this blockhead, idiot employee of mine," said Roy's former boss. "He wouldn't cut a few corners, and I had to fire him."

"Really?" said his friend. "Give me the guy's name."

The next day, the friend, who was a vice-president at another company, phoned Roy and asked if it was true he had refused to cut corners. "Yes, it's true," said Roy, "and I lost my job because of it."

The VP then said, "I'd like you to come in for an interview at my company—we want to hire people with integrity like yours." Roy landed a great job.

GAINING PERSONAL PERSPECTIVE

What basic principles of leadership did you gain from reading about Nehemiah's first days in Jerusalem?

_____

_____

_____

Which virtue in your life needs strengthening to keep your DICE boat from springing a leak?

_____

_____

_____

Can anyone learn to lead? Why or why not?

_____

_____

_____

Do you know of someone like Roy (or others in this chapter) who exercised virtue?

_____

_____

_____

Queen Esther: Refusing to Hide Behind Royalty

Nehemiah was not the first Jew to exhibit what we call Courageous Character before a Persian king. Thirty-five years earlier, King Xerxes (Artaxerxes' father) dismissed Queen Vashti for insubordination and crowned a Jewish woman named Esther in her place.

Despite Esther's elevation to royalty, this was one of the darkest hours in Jewish history. A nobleman named Haman tricked the king into permitting enemies of Jews across the Persian Empire to rise up and slaughter them on an appointed day. Queen Esther learned of the deception, but Persian law barred anyone, even the queen, from approaching the king without his summons. Violation of this law was punishable by death, except if the king chose to extend his golden scepter.

For the entire story, read the Old Testament Book of Esther.

To save her people, Esther took a public and risky stand by approaching the king without a summons. "If I die, I die," she concluded prior to entering the royal court. When he saw her, King Xerxes extended his scepter.

Esther boldly proclaimed her ethnicity and informed the king of Haman's evil plot to exterminate the Jews. As a result of her intervention, King Xerxes had Haman executed and gave Jews across the Persian Empire the right to mount a defense against their enemies.

By refusing to hide behind her royal robes and by advocating for a people sentenced to death, Queen Esther exhibited Courageous Character.

Mandela & de Klerk: Collaboration Demonstrated

The peaceful dismantling of the apartheid system in South Africa at the end of the twentieth century was made possible by the improbable collaboration of two political enemies: F. W. de Klerk and Nelson Mandela, who passed away December 5, 2013 at age 95. Between 1990 and 1994, the two men negotiated a political solution with the opportunity for democratic elections to replace the nation's racist laws.

De Klerk rose through the ranks of the white National Party, which enacted the apartheid laws in 1948. He became president of that party at the end of 1989. Mandela spent twenty-seven years in prison as a result of his activism against the apartheid laws, and was elected president of the black African National Congress (ANC) in July 1991.

Though dramatically different in their personal and political viewpoints, both men shared a common vision: change must happen in a peaceful and orderly fashion and that a united South Africa could be a better place for both blacks and whites. This shared vision helped bridge their differences and provided a platform for their collaboration (Dynamic Determination). Both understood the explosive nature of the issues they dealt with, possessed the mental capacity to imagine the possibilities beyond each political party's platform, worked hard to understand each other's point of view, and kept open minds (Intellectual Flexibility). While severely tested, Mandela and de Klerk considered each other to have sufficient personal integrity to trust one another and keep their promises. They risked all to do what they both agreed was the right thing (Courageous Character).

Finally, both possessed a high degree of self-confidence and emotional stability. When they displayed anger or frustration, they quickly repaired their relationship and came back to the negotiating table. They remained calm and resolute on the necessity of a peaceful transition when others on both sides were overcome by negative emotion. That solid determination at the top kept negotiations positive, hopeful, and for the most part moving forward (Emotional Maturity).

(continued on next page)

The two men faced many challenges:

Mandela had to persuade the majority blacks to remain patient and non-violent.

De Klerk had to persuade the minority whites that giving up their privileged status was in their self-interest.

Both had to persuade radical and violent elements in their own camps that the change process must happen in a peaceful and orderly manner. When violence flared, they remained calm and kept negotiations on track at considerable risk to their own political influence and to their very lives.

As a result of their collaboration, South Africa held its first national, nonracial, one-person-one-vote election on April 27, 1994. The ANC won just over 62 percent of the national vote and 252 of the 400 seats in the national assembly. Mandela was chosen the first black president of South Africa and de Klerk became deputy president of the coalition government. Power was peacefully transferred to the majority as the generals of the South African Defense Force and the police saluted Mandela and pledged their loyalty to the new government.

This dramatic and relatively peaceful shift in power was made possible in large part because two men, Nelson Mandela and F. W. de Klerk, chose to nurture a fruitful political partnership in the cause of national unity and democratic freedoms, and because both possessed the **DICE + 1** necessary to do so.

The partnership of these two unlikely collaborators, who in 1993 were jointly awarded the Nobel Peace Prize, gives us hope that when men and women empowered by a virtuous core are willing to take risks and overcome differences to pursue a noble cause, things previously thought impossible can happen.

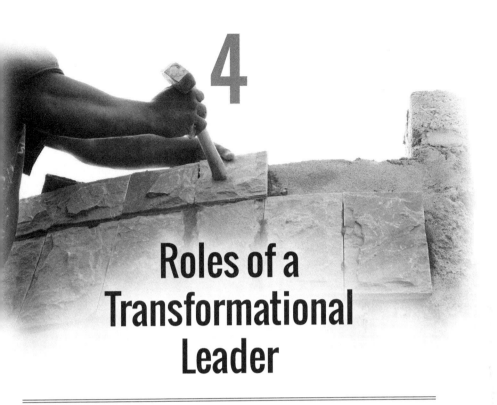

Roles of a Transformational Leader

The Ancient Text— The Book of Nehemiah 3:1-32

To the Reader: *Because the extensive listing of individuals, groups and occupations in this passage makes for difficult reading, we offer the following summary of this ancient text.*

Builders of the Wall

Priests serving in the temple led the effort to repair Jerusalem's walls. Whole families claimed sections of the walls adjacent to their houses. Other wall-workers streamed into the city from the countryside. Still other sections of the wall were rebuilt by trade groups like merchants, perfumers and goldsmiths. Nor was the effort accomplished only by men. Though writers of that era seldom mentioned women in lists of names, Nehemiah singled out a civil servant who he said "repaired the next section of wall with the help of his daughters."

Some volunteers repaired gates, roofing them over and setting their doors, bolts and bars in place. Others filled gaps in the walls. Still others reconstructed watch *towers strategically located between gates.*

Nehemiah recognized some who exerted extra effort in rebuilding Jerusalem's walls, like a man named Baruch who was said to have "zealously repaired" a section of the wall. He recognized others for their under-performance, like nobles of Tekoa who refused to join in the reconstruction project.

All told, thousands of individuals from inside and outside Jerusalem and from many walks of life came together with the single-minded goal of rebuilding the burned and broken gates and walls of this ancient city. Most had no prior construction experience. Many left behind their livelihoods to engage in this Herculean effort. All were committed to the task.

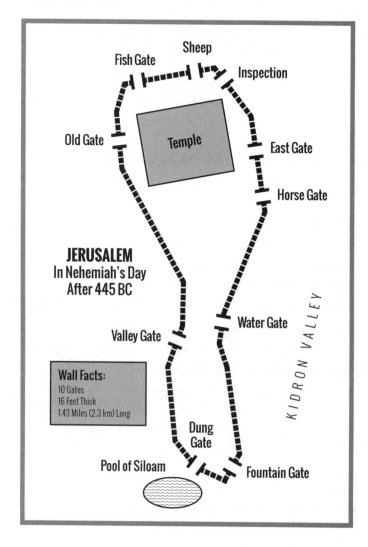

Nehemiah's Story Updated

To the despondent, dispirited citizens of Jerusalem, Nehemiah had cast a robust vision of a renewed, reborn community. For many of the city's residents, spiritual and social renewal began as they repaired the walls right in front of their homes. Jews in surrounding towns responded to the vision as well. Within days of Nehemiah spelling out his reconstruction strategy, forty-one teams of courageous men and women began work in a shared and well-coordinated effort to repair ten gates and forty-two sections of wall, each averaging 250 feet long and sixteen feet thick.

As Jotham had learned during his middle-of-the-night trek around the outside of the city with Nehemiah, the Babylonians had not destroyed the entire wall—just enough to render it useless as a defense.

Jotham watched in amazement as this diverse crew of amateur carpenters and masons launched themselves into the wall-rebuilding effort.

"None of these people are receiving pay for their labor, and yet each of them seems to be attacking the rebuilding effort as though they owned the wall," thought Jotham. Then it dawned on him. These people really do collectively own the wall. Nehemiah's role as a direction setter, responsible for Vision-Casting and Aligning Jerusalem's residents with what must to be done, had helped all of the wall-builders realize this truth. As a result, they were willing to contribute the extra effort required to turn that vision into reality.

Jotham dropped his pen and pad, and picked up a trowel.

About 80% of what it takes to lead transform-ationally is relational.

Four Roles Every Leader Must Play

As previously noted, the Relationships embedded in the acronym **DICE + 1** are the essential virtue-oriented capacities anyone must exhibit who wants to lead in a transformational manner. Relationships form the core of The 4-R Model because about 80 percent of what it takes to lead tranformationally is relational.

Beyond that core capacity, every person who aspires to transforma-

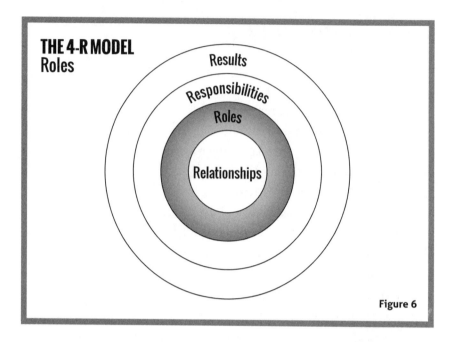

THE 4-R MODEL
Roles

Results

Responsibilities

Roles

Relationships

Figure 6

tional leadership must play four essential Roles. *See Figure 6.* These essential roles are Direction Setter, Spokesperson, Coach, and Change Agent.

Imagine that each of these four Roles is played in a separate arena—like a baseball diamond, a soccer field, a basketball court or a hockey rink. A leader will jump from one field of play to another as he leads transformationally. Over time he must play on all four fields. *See Figure 7.*

Two of the Roles (Direction Setter and Spokesperson) primarily interact with audiences outside an organization or group of followers, while two of the Roles (Coach and Change Agent) focus on inside audiences.

Two of the Roles (Direction Setter and Change Agent) relate primarily to the future of an organization or group of followers, and two of the Roles (Spokesperson and Coach) deal with the present.

The mandate for the leader in each Role is to develop a particular culture, a shared system of values within an organization or group of followers. Culture is "The way we do things around here." Every company, team, church, club, or family has a culture. Developing culture cannot be separated from the attitudes and behaviors of the leader. To use the language of the 4-R Model, developing a healthy and productive culture is an "inside out" process requiring the exercise of the leader's **DICE + 1**.

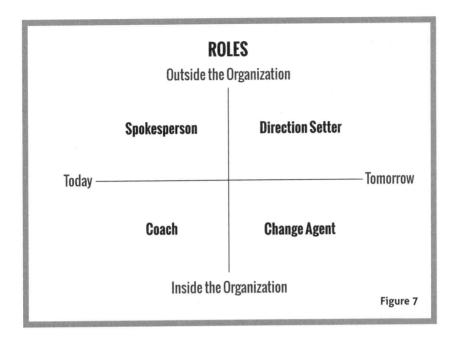

ROLES

Outside the Organization

Spokesperson | Direction Setter

Today —————————————————— Tomorrow

Coach | Change Agent

Inside the Organization

Figure 7

You may also have heard that "Culture eats strategy for breakfast!" No matter how well-conceived and communicated your strategy is, if you are bucking a cultural headwind, your strategy will have difficulty taking hold, if it takes hold at all. You may need to profoundly influence, and in some cases radically change, your culture in order for your strategies to succeed. The Roles of Direction Setter, Spokesperson, Coach and Change Agent help define culture. If leaders play them right, with strong **DICE + 1**, there is a good chance that culture can become a tailwind, giving their strategies an extra boost.

> If you let weeds grow under any of these leadership Roles your neglect will choke out your effectiveness.

Let's take a closer look at each of the four Roles of a Transformational Leader. Again, these are not the only Roles a leader will play, but they are the essential Roles every leader must play in order to lead transformationally. *But Be Warned: If you let weeds grow under any of these Roles—in other words, if you don't play each of these Roles with gusto—your neglect will choke out your effectiveness as a leader.*

THE DIRECTION SETTER ROLE–
An Outside Role Focused on the Future

In the Role of Direction Setter, the leader brings the people following him face-to-face with their identity and the unique mission of their association. He strives to answer two important questions: "Who are we?" and "What are we all about?"

A leader in the Direction Setter Role seeks to create a culture in which the identity of the organization is clearly articulated and his followers embrace it as their ultimate destiny. This Role is normally played within an organization, but it is considered an external Role because it is focused on serving the customer by:

We use customer in the broad sense of the word. Customers may be clients of a non-profit organization, employees of a company, or even members of a family.

- *Shaping, clarifying, and defining the core values of the organization.*

- *Shaping, clarifying, and defining the unique mission of the organization.*

- *Integrating the core values and mission* into each of the other three Role playing areas of the leader's life: Spokesperson, Coach, and Change Agent.

The marks of a genuinely mission-driven organization include:

- *A deep customer focus.* Transformational organizations, whether companies or families, do not exist for themselves. They have been called into existence to serve. The mission-driven organization is defined by a deep and abiding sense that it exists for the welfare of others.

- *A future orientation.* Mission-driven communities lean into the future. They are committed to serving customers over time and in a variety of conditions.

Our ancient friend Nehemiah played the Direction Setter Role when he faced the residents of Jerusalem for the very first time, reminding them that God had promised to bring his chosen people back to Jerusalem to live in relationship with Him. This vision for the future was deeply rooted in values Nehemiah had gleaned as a student of the Hebrew Scriptures. In the Role of Direction Setter, he cast a vision for rebuilding the city walls and the morale of this defeated people, and eventually their entire community. Securing the city was a necessary first step to returning to the covenant life God had prepared for them.

It may appear that Nehemiah was addressing insiders, but remember that he was a newcomer to Jerusalem. The people to whom he articulated his vision were residents of a city which had been overrun by its enemies for 140 years. They had no allegiance to newly appointed Governor Nehemiah. He was an outsider. As he talked, however, the residents of Jerusalem coalesced around his message which centered on their shared values and the future God had promised them.

By the time Nehemiah finished speaking, many of those listening began to own the mission and values. "Let us start rebuilding," they replied in unison. In the days to come, Nehemiah would also play Coach and Change Agent as he led these people in the wall-building effort. To those slow to respond or who opposed the vision, Nehemiah would continue to define the deep identity of the culture he proposed or serve in the Role of Spokesperson. We will explore these Roles in greater detail, later in this chapter.

★ ★ ★

In their book *Built to Last*, leadership researchers Jim Collins and Jerry Porras discuss the attributes shared by hundred-year old companies that have weathered depressions, recessions and business cycles, and kept on growing. These two attributes stand out:

1. *They have deeply and widely held core values* that are woven into the fabric of their organizational culture—standards that keep them upright as the deep roots of a tree hold it upright in a storm.

2. *They lean into the future.* In other words, they have a clear mission or unique purpose that drives them forward.

A prime example is Johnson & Johnson, whose Tylenol brand commanded the lion's share (37 percent) of the over-the-counter pain reliever market in 1982. In the fall of that year, someone removed several bottles of

Tylenol capsules from retail shelves in the Chicago area, laced the capsules with deadly cyanide, and replaced them. Seven people were reported to have died after taking the extra-strength Tylenol capsules.

Johnson & Johnson immediately ceased all Tylenol advertising, recalled thirty-one million bottles of extra strength capsules at a cost of over $100 million.

At the time, I (Jim) was heavily involved in selling Procter & Gamble brands in the marketplace. Johnson & Johnson was a very worthy competitor, and I was shocked to learn they were taking Tylenol off the market. Tylenol was responsible for 19 percent of Johnson & Johnson's corporate profits during the first three quarters of 1982. The product accounted for 13 percent of Johnson & Johnson's year-to-year sales growth and 33 percent of the company's year-to-year profit growth. *"Couldn't they find a solution while they continued to market the brand?"* I wondered.

Less than six months after the crisis occurred, Johnson & Johnson brought Tylenol back to the retail shelves with a new triple safety seal packaging—a glued box, a plastic seal over the neck of the bottle, and a foil seal over the mouth of the bottle. It became the first product in the industry to use the new tamper-resistant packaging.

Tylenol recovered all its share loss and continues to be a very strong brand. The 1982 Tylenol episode is heralded as a crisis communication masterpiece, and then CEO James Burke was highly acclaimed for leading the Tylenol communication and rebuilding plan. But behind the scenes was the company's "Credo."

Written in 1943 just before Johnson & Johnson became publicly traded, the Credo is a statement of the company's values. A critical responsibility of every Johnson & Johnson CEO is to ensure the Credo is woven into the fabric of the organization, is understood, and is being followed by all entities and employees. The Credo begins with these words:

> *"We believe our first responsibility is to the doctors, nurses, and patients, to mothers and fathers and all others who use our products and services. In meeting their needs everything we do must be of high quality. We must constantly strive to reduce our costs in order to maintain reasonable prices. Customers' orders must be serviced promptly and accurately. Our suppliers and distributors must have an opportunity to make a fair profit."*

Clearly, these values, deeply understood by the entire company, guided the initial reactions and decisions about how to handle this incredibly difficult product liability and corporate image crisis.

Compare the Tylenol scandal to the issues surrounding the Pinto in the '70s when Ford used a cost/benefit analysis to determine whether or not to fix a known fire risk with the Pinto's gas tank, or the 2001 Ford/Firestone fight over shredding tires and Explorer roll-overs. In the latter case, evidence indicates both were at fault: the tires manufactured in Firestone's Decatur, Illinois plants were sub-standard and the Ford Explorer was prone to roll-overs.

Instead of acting to protect the consumer, each company blamed the other for the problem. In the end, they refused to do business together, despite a long-standing customer-supplier relationship—Henry Ford and Harvey Firestone were best of friends.

Each of the above situations could have had a much better outcome if the organizations involved had been guided by clear values deeply embedded in their cultures.

THE SPOKESPERSON ROLE–
An Outside Role Focused on the Here and Now

If the Direction Setter Role clarifies who the organization aspires to serve and how it can serve them, the Spokesperson is about actually delivering that service. In the Role of Spokesperson, a leader seeks to create a culture in which customers are connected with the organization's people and resources, these connections are expanded, and customer-service is given the right-of-way in the daily life of the organization.

To lead an organization or a group that stays connected with its customers, the Spokesperson must focus on two big things:

1. *Shaping a customer-friendly culture.*

2. *Protecting the organization and its people from irrelevance by his or her personal engagement with customers.*

The marks of a customer-engaged organization include:

- *Spending time learning and understanding customer needs.* Customer-engaged organizations are trusted because they listen.

- *Becoming indispensable to its customers.* Customer-engaged organizations enjoy strong partnerships with those they serve.

- *Dealing honestly with issues.* Customer-engaged organizations experience a paradoxical blend of welcome and discomfort, attraction and repulsion. They're okay with being loved and hated at the same time.

The Consumer is Boss

During my career with Procter & Gamble, I (Jim) watched its leadership go the extra mile to shape a consumer-friendly culture. A.G. Lafley, the company's CEO from 2000 to 2010, visited consumers' homes once a month to observe how they used P&G products and to learn how we could improve. That set the tone for the rest of us to follow his mantra: "The consumer is boss."

> The Spokesperson's Role is by far the most rigorous and least popular Role every leader must play.

P&G also pioneered Customer Business Development (CBD) where we worked in multi-functional teams with our customers. P&G formed the first CBD team with Wal-Mart in the late 1980s. Until that time, the standard interaction between P&G and its customers involved the salesperson/buyer interface. The salesperson called on the buyer, the buyer took the news back to a committee, and the committee made a decision. Hopefully, the customer placed an order.

Recognizing that enormous non-value-added costs existed throughout the consumer products value chain, and realizing more sales could be gained through collaboration, Wal-Mart and P&G pioneered a team-based approach. In addition to sales, these teams included logistics, operations, finance, marketing, category management, and information systems.

These multi-functional teams significantly streamlined the value chain, creating supply chain, warehousing, shelf stock, and merchandising efficiencies that reduced product cost for Wal-Mart. It enabled the retailer to deliver on its tagline, "Always Low Prices." Customer Business Development was—and is—a great success and an excellent example of developing a "customer-friendly" culture.

Dealing Honestly with the Issues

None of the four leadership Roles is easy. While the Spokesperson's part is no more technically challenging than any other Role, it is by far the most rigorous—and at times the most dangerous. As such it is the least popular Role every transformational leader must play. Nehemiah can testify to this fact.

Addressing the residents of Jerusalem for the first time, Nehemiah played two leadership Roles. As Direction Setter, he affirmed the Jews' identity and purpose as God's chosen people and their opportunity to rebuild their community and their covenant relationship with God. At the same time, Nehemiah played the Role of Spokesperson. He addressed those assembled in the manner of an ambassador addressing a foreign government. He was an outsider. As yet he had no followers and no one had signed onto his vision. But that did not stop him from dealing honestly with the issues.

Since arriving from Susa, he had listened carefully and learned much. Now as he spoke, Nehemiah sought to connect with his audience. No doubt he reminded the Jews how their ancestors had been taken into captivity by the Babylonians. He pointed to their current condition—Jerusalem in ruins and gates burned. He identified with the people, including himself in the assessment. "You see the trouble we are in?"

Nehemiah spoke both honestly and graciously. He talked about the people's current disgrace, which was probably not something they liked to hear. But his talk of God's favor and the king's support stirred their hearts and gave them hope.

"Let us start rebuilding," they responded, and many followed Nehemiah to the wall, as evidenced by the description of the construction teams and the plans detailed in the ancient text. But not everyone cheered the Spokesperson that day.

Though he was authorized and supported by the King of Persia, the former cup-bearer faced strident opposition from leaders of nearby tribes. Sanballat the Horonite, Tobiah the Ammonite, and Geshem the Arab initially tried to intimidate Nehemiah by insinuating that he and the Jews were rebelling against the king. They eventually threatened violence against the construction effort and against Nehemiah personally. Nehemiah would never become a popular public figure with the surrounding nations, and he remained unpopular with many in Jerusalem to the end of his career.

Popularity means that, for the moment and for whatever reason, people find a leader appealing. But popularity will never ensure the kind of deep and permanent relevance that is the intersection between the customer and the organization—between the person in need and what the organization offers. On the other hand, lack of popularity does not mean a loss of credibility. It simply means that, for the moment, the Spokesperson has attracted the attention of those who are not yet prepared to respond to the purpose and vision of the organization.

So Spokesperson is the Role with the most stress and the one that takes the most heat. Think of William Wilberforce who endured forty years of rejection before colleagues in Parliament finally abolished slavery. Think of Johnson & Johnson CEO James Burke who faced both the news media and the general public after the 1982 Tylenol poisonings. Think of any press secretary in recent memory who faces a roomful of reporters after his president's comments stir up a media hornet's nest. Not surprisingly, this Spokesperson Role demands the full capacities of the **DICE + 1** leader.

As Nehemiah demonstrated, it takes a deep sense of inner strength linked to a greater purpose in life (Dynamic Determination) to play the Role of Spokesperson, bringing both healing and division. It also takes a high level of personal security (Emotional Maturity) for a transformational leader to accept being both deeply loved and just as deeply hated—warmly embraced and bitterly rejected.

Having settled issues of self-esteem, identity, and power, the transformational leader can heed the advice of the ancient Arab proverb: "The dogs bark but the caravan moves on." Humility and seeing clearly requires the leader to listen to some critics, but he makes a distinction between benefactors and detractors whose "carping" is as relevant as a dog barking at the wheels of a car.

THE COACH ROLE–
An Inside Role Focused on the Here and Now

A leader playing the essential Role of Coach channels the talent and resources of the community into productive patterns of mission-driven activity. As part of this process, the Coach must speak to the emotional needs of his followers. This may be the most difficult task involved in playing this Role.

The Coach also "sweats" the need for new generations of **DICE + 1** leaders to live out an organization's core values and move it toward fulfillment of its mission.

To keep the organization focused on its mission, in the present and into the future, the Coach must concentrate on two big things:

1. *Fostering the development of the mission-driven organization by shaping a leadership-friendly culture.*

2. *Executing a leadership pipeline process.* If the organization is to increase its capacity to serve customers, it must perfect its ability to identify, develop, and deploy the next generation of leaders.

Leadership-Friendly Cultures

Organizations with leader-friendly cultures:

• *Believe that vast, untapped leadership potential resides in followers who have yet to be identified or to prove themselves in their own spheres of influence.*

• *Believe that established leaders must serve and lead in a way that secures the next generation of leaders.*

• *Value personal development in the context of the organization's mission.*

Playing the Role of Coach, Nehemiah transformed the residents of Jerusalem, who embraced the vision of a restored community, into a well-organized construction crew. He seemed to have identified and assigned them to tasks for which they were fit and which would give them a sense of accomplishment and ownership in the wall-building effort. Nothing is said about organizing them by their experience. There were no experienced wall-builders in Jerusalem.

Family or occupational groups—and sometimes proximity to the gate or section of wall being rebuilt—seemed to play the biggest part in the construction assignments handed out by the new governor. Eliashib the high priest and his fellow priests were the first to be assigned. They rebuilt the Sheep Gate. Others, like Jedaiah son of Harumaph, made repairs to the wall opposite their houses. Perhaps Nehemiah distributed these duties with an eye toward encouraging the wall-builders. They would either be working with others of like interests or building sections of the wall close to their places of residence for which they could take ownership.

In any case, Nehemiah's work assignments appear strategically brilliant. Great coaches are renowned for their ability to inspire and encourage.

As the often injured, former football great Joe Namath observed, "When you win, nothing hurts." Or to paraphrase the German philosopher Nietzsche, a person can endure almost any "what" if he has a "why". Nehemiah inspired the residents of Jerusalem by offering them their first taste of winning for over a century—their motivational "why".

Consequently, men and women temporarily abandoned their means of earning a living to focus on rebuilding the wall. They went the extra mile, doing not only what was required but also what was necessary for the success of the endeavor.

But inspiration will not always see a transformational mission through to completion. Their enemies plotted a surprise attack on the Jews rebuilding Jerusalem's walls. At this point, the Jews had built the wall to half height, but they ceased building in the face of fierce opposition and weariness. They needed encouragement. Nehemiah spoke to the emotional needs of the workers by appealing to their belief in an all-powerful God and their love of family. "Don't be afraid of the enemy," he urged those working on the wall. "Remember the Lord who is great and glorious, and fight for your brothers, your sons, your daughters, your wives, and your homes."

The ancient text records that, when their enemies learned their plot had been discovered and that God had frustrated it, the workers resumed the rebuilding effort.

A Leadership Pipeline

The acid test of leadership is the legacy one leaves behind. A vision of great worth is rarely accomplished in the brief span of one generation. Unless the leader's vision and values can be transferred to the next generation, the organization will likely fail.

Besides organizing, inspiring, and encouraging the workers, Nehemiah identified and developed leaders to carry on after him. Later in the ancient text, the new governor gave instructions to the people he had placed in authority—officers, builders and helpers—as they defended the half-built wall against attack. When the rebuilding effort concluded, Nehemiah dedicated the walls and filled key leadership positions. He appointed his brother Hanani and Hananiah, the commander of the fortress protecting the city, to be in charge of Jerusalem. Nehemiah himself eventually returned to Susa.

> **The acid test of leadership is the legacy one leaves behind.**

Sometime later, he again asked King Artaxerxes for permission to travel to Jerusalem. What he found greatly troubled him. Many of the city's leaders, including some Nehemiah had personally appointed, had been negligent in his absence. They allowed the city's residents to engage in evil behavior of the sort that had led to the Jews being overrun by the Babylonians and sent into exile. So Nehemiah selected and appointed new leaders.

Transformational leaders are concerned about the next generation of leaders. The Role of Coach focuses all its resources on the discovery and development of men and women who will live out an organization's core values and move it toward fulfillment of its mission.

Kevin Wilde, vice president of organizational effectiveness and chief learning officer at General Mills, affirms the value of the coach in advancing tomorrow's leaders. "In studying the managers who have moved from good to great, we uncovered that coaching was the major improvement," says Wilde. "Over time, our leaders became better managers of their employees primarily by extending their coaching." So General Mills, an international food company that has paid dividends to investors for over a hundred years, launched a series of Great Manager Coaching training programs globally and has trained over one thousand leaders.

"Just as a chef returns to the kitchen after serving a great meal, we keep refining the leadership development recipe," says Wilde of the company's constant search for next generation leadership.

"We must be constantly weaving into our organization the new generation," said John R. Mott, longtime YMCA leader and winner of the 1946

Nobel Peace prize. "He who does the work is not so profitably employed as he who multiplies the doers. Count the day lost that you do not do something, either directly or indirectly, to multiply the number of unselfish workers."

THE CHANGE AGENT ROLE–
An Inside Role Focused on the Future

The Direction Setter establishes clarity as to the mission and purpose of an organization, and the Change Agent establishes a culture of learning that increases, over time, its effectiveness in striving for that mission and purpose.

To accomplish this, a leader in the Role of Change Agent must focus on two big things:

1. *Fostering the development of a mission-driven community by shaping a learning culture.*

2. *Prompting and supporting a process of constructive change and continuous learning.*

A learning community is one which:

• *Seeks effective solutions to critical, mission-related problems.*
  Members of the community learn how to learn together about the things that matter most.

• *Practices new learning,* expanding the community's capacity to thrive in new and dynamic environments—and to change those environments.

• *Distinguishes progress toward its mission from mere change.*
  It embraces the future without losing what is of value from the past.

Our Middle-Eastern example, Nehemiah, modeled a culture of continuous learning and constructive change, before and during the wall-rebuilding effort.

Traveling to Jerusalem for the very first time, Nehemiah had the king's blessing and army with him. Yet he did not flaunt his power to make decisions or assume his was the only way of doing things.

Instead, Nehemiah traveled around the city anonymously, by night, inspecting the damaged wall and gathering information on what would be needed to repair it. Then, instead of issuing an edict, which the new governor had every right to do, Nehemiah presented to Jerusalem's leaders the opportunity which lay before them all to restore the city's security. No doubt the unveiling of his plan to change the status quo carried more credibility with the city's residents because he had actually walked through the gaping holes in the wall and touched the gates burned with fire.

This policy of continuous learning and constructive change continued as repairs to the wall progressed. Several times their enemies sought to impede the work. Eventually they threatened ambush. "Before they know what's happening, we will swoop down on them and kill them and end their work," said their enemies.

Upon learning of this plot, Nehemiah split the original construction crews into two groups: one to stand guard and the other to continue the work. He was constantly learning and making adjustments of the kind that would allow the mission to continue in an ever-changing environment.

Nehemiah could have brought the favor of the king and the power of the king's army to bear on the Jews' enemies, but that would have ignored the principles on which this mission was founded—that God, not the king, had decreed that this was the point in history at which the wall would be rebuilt and the community of Jerusalem restored. In realigning his workforce and trusting God to protect the wall-building effort, Nehemiah embraced the future without losing what was of value from the past.

Nehemiah's example stands in stark contrast to many of the decisions made on the battlefield by Union and Confederate generals during the U.S. Civil War. In battle after battle, the generals ordered their soldiers to charge in rank file, only to be mowed down by cannon and rifle fire. Tens of thousands died at Gettysburg, Chancellorsville, Fredericksburg, Shiloh, and many other battles because the generals continued to use war tactics developed decades earlier, despite improvements to weapons.

Following the Mexican War of 1848, weapons manufacturers significantly improved the range and accuracy of rifles and greatly advanced the range, accuracy, and type of shot used in cannons. As a result, gunners and artillery men could mow down the ranks of oncoming enemy soldiers. Rather than adjust their tactics to accommodate this new technology, generals on both sides continued to send their troops forward, battle after battle, and day after day, to be chopped down by a hail of gunfire and withering artillery barrages. Pickett's Charge, on the third day of the Battle of Gettysburg (Pennsylvania) stands as the most striking example of this failure to learn and adapt. On July 3, 1863, 12,500 Confederates charged across an open field to attack the Union forces. When the battle ended, half of these Confederate soldiers lay dead or wounded as a result of their leaders' futile attempt to breach the Union lines.

Fast forward fifty-three years to the start of World War I in Europe. In 1914, tactics still had not changed despite even more improvements in artillery and the advent of the machine gun. Generals, especially the French and the British, ordered their men to attack enemy lines fortified by entrenched artillery and machine gun nests. They fought battle after battle and accomplished almost nothing except adding to the list of casualties. At best, they gained a few hundred yards of ground before being pushed back.

In particular, British General Douglas Haig gained notoriety due to his inability to grasp modern tactics and adjust to changes in weapon technology. Early in the conflict, Haig declared that the war would be won or lost by cavalry, but soldiers on horseback proved irrelevant to the outcome of World War I. Forces under "Butcher Haig," as he became known, sustained needlessly heavy casualties over the course of the war.

GM v. Toyota: Ignoring v. Changing

Playing the Change Agent Role is extremely important and required. Lives, jobs, and whole organizations can be lost because leaders fail to play this Role. Consider General Motors. At one point, they had a huge share of the U.S. automobile market. Many believed GM cars and trucks to be the best the world had to offer.

Enter Dr. W. Edwards Deming, a highly educated engineer with graduate degrees in mathematics and physics. After World War II, Deming worked under General Douglas MacArthur on the reconstruction of Japan. He began teaching Japanese business leaders statistical process control as a way of driving quality throughout a manufacturing system. The idea was to measure each step of the system so that each step, as well as the entire process, produced "total quality."

Eiji Toyoda, architect of the Toyota Motor Company, adopted Deming's quality concepts and began to perfect the metrics and processes necessary to build quality into every aspect of the automobile manufacturing process. Toyota entered the U.S. market in the late 1950s with limited success, but then succeeded in the late 1960s with the Toyota Corolla, which became the world's best-selling car. Toyota continued to gain share of U.S. and global markets by consistently making changes necessary to deliver reliable, high quality cars and trucks that met consumer needs.

Lives, jobs, and entire organizations can be lost because leaders fail to play the Change Agent Role.

Early on, General Motors had dismissed Toyota as a minor irritant. GM did not adopt rigorous quality standards and continued to make cars like they always had. Their lack of quality was exposed when compared with the products coming from Japan. Later, GM would apologize for the quality of the cars they sold in the 1980s. GM went from being a trusted U.S. brand to a suspect brand, while the Japanese began to be seen as reliability and quality leaders.

As Toyota and other Japanese automakers gained market share, they took a lot of heat for their success. GM and other domestic manufacturers complained about the need for tariffs to level the playing field. To quiet the tariff tempest, Toyota offered to partner with GM and teach their quality process to the American automaker. Toyota and GM formed a joint-venture company, New United Motor Manufacturing (NUMMI).

NUMMI re-opened a GM plant in Oakland, California that had been a problem due to drugs, absenteeism, and other personnel problems. The company began producing Toyota Corollas and Chevrolet Prizms. Under Toyota's tutelage, the plant turned around. Productivity significantly improved as did the quality of the cars manufactured. Although the Corolla and the Prizm were essentially the same car, Corollas greatly outsold Prizms, another indication of how much brand equity GM had lost with the American consumer.

Working hand in hand with a company that had mastered continuous improvement should have been a boon to GM. Here was an opportunity to learn the widely acclaimed Toyota Production System.

Ignoring the opportunity to improve the quality and reliability of their cars using Total Quality principles, GM chose instead to focus on the production of trucks, including investing over a $1 billion on the Hummer brand. Rising fuel prices, the recession, the corresponding drop in truck sales, inefficient branding and marketing, and lack of an energy efficient vehicle (like the Prius) to fall back on caused GM to end up in Washington, D.C. asking for a bail-out to stave off bankruptcy. They got their bailout, at the taxpayers' expense, and left with a haircut—four brands gone and the management team fired.

But GM is coming back, thanks to solid leadership willing to make hard choices and play the Change Agent Role. For decades, GM managed rather than led. For all practical purposes, they ignored the Change Agent Role. At the very least, they failed to make the hard leadership decisions needed to stem their share losses and recover their business by meeting the needs of a fast-changing marketplace.

Leaders who ignore the Change Agent Role do so at their own peril. Lives, jobs, and whole organizations can be lost as a result.

Bring Your Best DICE + 1 to Each Role

A leader's effectiveness in playing each of the previously mentioned four Roles is directly related to the traits of consequence and the ability to collaborate, the **DICE + 1**, that he or she brings to the playing field. *See Figure 8.*

Drawing from the trait of Dynamic Determination, the Direction Setter infuses the organization with faith in its larger purpose, hope to sustain its progress in difficult times, and courage to live out its values and persevere in the face of opposition. Without Dynamic Determination, the leader will likely have difficulty clarifying the mission of the organization

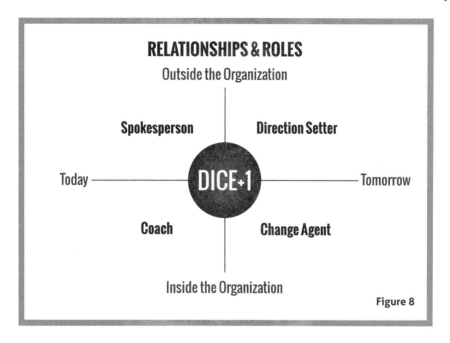

RELATIONSHIPS & ROLES
Outside the Organization

Spokesperson   Direction Setter

Today — DICE+1 — Tomorrow

Coach   Change Agent

Inside the Organization

Figure 8

which serves as the foundation for sustained, collaborative effort.

A Change Agent draws from the trait of Intellectual Flexibility to stay humble, teachable, and open to new learning. She will keep exploring and discovering new ways of thinking and behaving, and readily change her mind when presented with evidence that challenges or overrules established convictions. Fueled by Intellectual Flexibility, she will be quick to unlearn and break behavior patterns that no longer add value to the organization. A leader who lacks Intellectual Flexibility is likely to become rigid and fail to embrace new ways to improve the organization's performance.

Drawing from the trait of Courageous Character, the leader as Spokesperson exercises the moral courage required to transcend self-interest and extend the organization's resources outward to deliver something of value, something of benefit for others. The Spokesperson with strong Courageous Character seeks the welfare and best interests of others, even in the face of inconvenience, and at times at great personal sacrifice. Lacking moral courage, a leader is likely to become insular, indifferent, and disconnected from the needs of those the organization says it wants to serve.

Exhibiting the trait of Emotional Maturity, a Coach offers a rare blend of boldness and generosity. He creates something of value—a winning team or effective organization—and willingly shares it with emerging leaders, eventually surrendering control over that which he himself has produced to the next generation. Lacking Emotional Maturity, a leader in the Coach Role is likely to hoard leadership prerogatives, and withhold personal support and resources from new leaders, thereby stifling their growth. The organization is diminished as talented and capable adults are denied what they need to grow.

While the traits mentioned above seem especially useful to the Roles with which we have paired them, do not be complacent. Anyone who aspires to lead in a transformational manner must bring all of the **DICE** to the playing of each Role, if they want to be successful. If you are not Intellectually Flexible—if you seem to be a know-it-all and rigid in your thinking—it will be very hard for people to follow long-term in any of the Roles—not just Change Agent. You'll weary them.

Likewise, if you're not Dynamically Determined as a leader—if I can't count on you to keep going when the going gets tough—then I will have a hard time following you in any of the Roles—not just Direction Setter. As leadership author and speaker John Maxwell points out, "He who thinks he leads, but has no followers, is only taking a walk."

To be an effective transformational leader, people must be able to follow you whatever Role you are playing, because of who you are—not because of your position. That will only happen as you exhibit strength in all four traits of consequence so that you possess the capacity to collaborate effectively. By bringing your best **DICE + 1** you are positively impacting and leveraging the culture for which each Role takes responsibility.

GAINING PERSONAL PERSPECTIVE

Why does it take DICE + 1 configuration of virtue to play each Role? For instance, what DICE components are required to play Coach or Change Agent?

_____

_____

_____

_____

Are you drawn to a particular Role? Why?

_____

_____

_____

_____

Is there a particular Role you find especially difficult? Why?

_____

_____

_____

_____

5

Responsibilities of a Transformational Leader

The Ancient Text—The Book of Nehemiah 4:1-23

Enemies Oppose the Rebuilding

¹Sanballat was very angry when he learned that we were rebuilding the wall. He flew into a rage and mocked the Jews, ²saying in front of his friends and the Samarian army officers, "What does this bunch of poor, feeble Jews think they're doing? Do they think they can build the wall in a single day by just offering a few sacrifices? Do they actually think they can make something of stones from a rubbish heap—and charred ones at that?"

³Tobiah the Ammonite, who was standing beside him, remarked, "That stone wall would collapse if even a fox walked along the top of it!"

⁴Then I prayed, "Hear us, our God, for we are being mocked. May their scoffing fall back on their own heads, and may they themselves become captives in a foreign land! ⁵Do not ignore their guilt. Do not blot out their sins, for they have provoked you to anger here in front of the builders."

⁶At last the wall was completed to half its height around the entire city, for the people had worked with enthusiasm.

⁷ *But when Sanballat and Tobiah and the Arabs, Ammonites, and Ashdodites heard that the work was going ahead and that the gaps in the wall of Jerusalem were being repaired, they were furious.* ⁸ *They all made plans to come and fight against Jerusalem and throw us into confusion.* ⁹ *But we prayed to our God and guarded the city day and night to protect ourselves.*

¹⁰ *Then the people of Judah began to complain, "The workers are getting tired, and there is so much rubble to be moved. We will never be able to build the wall by ourselves."*

¹¹ *Meanwhile, our enemies were saying, "Before they know what's happening, we will swoop down on them and kill them and end their work."*

¹² *The Jews who lived near the enemy came and told us again and again, "They will come from all directions and attack us!"* ¹³ *So I placed armed guards behind the lowest parts of the wall in the exposed areas. I stationed the people to stand guard by families, armed with swords, spears, and bows.*

¹⁴ *Then as I looked over the situation, I called together the nobles and the rest of the people and said to them, "Don't be afraid of the enemy! Remember the Lord, who is great and glorious, and fight for your brothers, your sons, your daughters, your wives, and your homes!"*

¹⁵ *When our enemies heard that we knew of their plans and that God had frustrated them, we all returned to our work on the wall.* ¹⁶ *But from then on, only half my men worked while the other half stood guard with spears, shields, bows, and coats of mail. The leaders stationed themselves behind the people of Judah* ¹⁷ *who were building the wall. The laborers carried on their work with one hand supporting their load and one hand holding a weapon.* ¹⁸ *All the builders had a sword belted to their side. The trumpeter stayed with me to sound the alarm.*

¹⁹ *Then I explained to the nobles and officials and all the people, "The work is very spread out, and we are widely separated from each other along the wall.* ²⁰ *When you hear the blast of the trumpet, rush to wherever it is sounding. Then our God will fight for us!"*

²¹ *We worked early and late, from sunrise to sunset. And half the men were always on guard.* ²² *I also told everyone living outside the walls to stay in Jerusalem. That way they and their servants could help with guard duty at night and work during the day.* ²³ *During this time, none of us—not I, nor my relatives, nor my servants, nor the guards who were with me—ever took off our clothes. We carried our weapons with us at all times, even when we went for water.*

Nehemiah's Story Updated

Jotham put down his trowel and wiped the sweat from his brow. He and the others had made good progress. Most of the 140-year-old breaches in Jerusalem's outer wall had been rebuilt to half their height. But the builders were bushed. Carrying mortar and lifting heavy stones day after day took a physical toll on the construction crews, especially the perfumers and goldsmiths. Even more draining were the constant taunts and threats of their enemies who reportedly planned an armed assault on the builders of the wall. Everyone feared the worst.

But two things kept the workers going:

- First, Jotham's friend and mentor Nehemiah had converted half the workforce into an army to stand between the workers and an attack from the outside. This offered hope that the enemies of this project might be repelled.

- Second, Nehemiah had reminded the workers of their purpose for rebuilding the wall and encouraged them to trust in God, who had already shown himself strong by giving them the king's favor. "Remember the Lord who is great and awesome and fight for your families…our God will fight for us."

Jotham knew these were not empty words. In the days since Nehemiah arrived in Jerusalem and shared his vision, the citizens who responded had come to respect the new governor for his devotion to God, for his courage, and for his compassion. He could have holed up in the governor's house and sent his orders via underlings. Instead, Nehemiah stood along with the workers at the wall—laboring with them and now guarding them from their enemies. He wouldn't even break from his vigilance long enough to change clothes during this tense time of anticipated assault.

Encouraged by Nehemiah's strong personal example, as well as the strategic changes he had made in their defense, the workers returned to the wall with renewed physical and emotional resolve.

Jotham picked up his trowel and kept going.

What Every Leader Must Do

In Chapter 3, we said that a person aspiring to transformational leadership must exhibit four virtue-based traits referred to collectively as **DICE**: Dynamic Determinism, Intellectual Flexibility, Courageous Character and Emotional Maturity. As a leader's **DICE** level increases, so does his ability to form and grow collaborative Relationships with a diverse array of people over time and in a variety of situations. We call that his Collaborative Quotient or **+ 1**. That ability to collaborate, added to a leader's **DICE**, is referred to as his **DICE + 1** capacity.

We proposed, in Chapter 4, that anyone aspiring to transformational leadership must bring her best **DICE + 1** to the playing of four essential Roles: Direction Setter, Spokesperson, Coach, and Change Agent. We pictured these Roles as four quadrants created by drawing a horizontal and a vertical axis, with the leader constantly moving from one quadrant or playing field to another.

Responsibilities form the third ring of 4-R Model. *See Figure 9.* There are many things a leader might do as he plays the essential Roles, but every

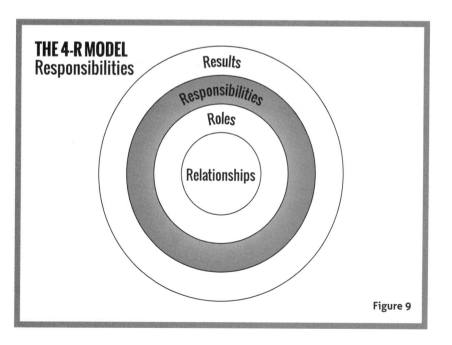

Figure 9

transformational leader must engage in certain essential activities over time. This chapter will expand on four essential activities or Responsibilities: Vision-Casting, Strategy-Making, Aligning, and Encouraging. *See Figure 10.*

The 4-R Model of Leadership describes these Responsibilities as having ongoing action. They are cyclical, suggesting continuous, forward momentum. Vision-Casting generates the momentum, Strategy-Making organizes a framework for the momentum, Aligning releases the momentum into that framework, and Encouraging sustains the momentum. Since the world is ever changing, the transformational leader must continually engage in Vision-Casting, so the cycle repeats itself.

The model also pictures these essential Responsibilities against the four Role quadrants, since a leader must engage in Vision-Casting, Strategy-Making, Aligning, and Encouraging as he plays each of the four roles.

Let's take a closer look at each of these Responsibilities and how our ancient friend Nehemiah carried out each of them.

VISION-CASTING

The process of Vision-Casting involves shaping and communicating a compelling and transforming picture of a preferable future that most any-

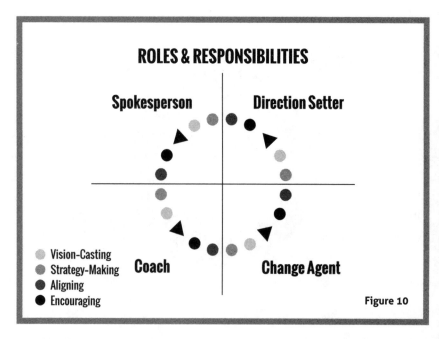

Figure 10

one can understand and that many are willing to embrace. Vision-Casting is the most important Responsibility of a transformational leader and is what separates leaders from managers. A manager focuses on what needs to be done today, but a leader focuses on tomorrow.

Nehemiah's journey started on his knees, in prayer. The cupbearer, being informed by his study of Jewish history and his relationship with God, received his vision of what could be done to address his people's brokenness and discouragement. Now he had to communicate that vision, to rebuild the community starting with rebuilding the wall.

STRATEGY-MAKING

Without a way to bring a vision to reality, it remains just a dream. Strategy-Making, the second Responsibility of a transformational leader, connects the present reality with the desired future by creating a workable structure or plan within which people can act to bring about the vision.

Concerning the Jews in the fifth century BC, Nehemiah researched and developed a strategy to bring about the vision. He did part of his Strategy-Making before traveling to Jerusalem, as indicated by his request for the king to provide timber for the city gates. He put the finishing touches on his strategy and the tactics required to bring it about during a middle-of-the-night journey around Jerusalem's compromised wall. Soon afterwards, Nehemiah shared that strategy with city leaders as part of communicating the vision. "Come, let us rebuild the wall...," he said, "and we will no longer be in disgrace."

A well-devised strategy answers the question: "How can we best utilize our precious resources (people, money, time, and leadership attention) to realize our vision?" Nehemiah's strategy called for full-time efforts of all who signed onto the vision. By leaving their occupations and concentrating their attention on the rebuilding the wall, these novice construction workers fortified the city in just fifty-two days and avoided interference by neighboring tribes who appeared to be taken by surprise at their progress. Perhaps they were surprised by the passion with which the Jews attacked the work, compared to their previous passivity.

It is important to note that transformational leaders must remain humbly engaged and give themselves permission to get smarter and adjust strategy over time. Under threat of armed opposition, Nehemiah changed his strategy, converting half of the workers into a militia that stood guard while the other half built the wall.

ALIGNING

The third Responsibility of a transformational leader is Aligning, which involves releasing a community's resources, especially human and financial, to get them moving toward their future. To accomplish this, a leader must evoke in followers who will actually be doing the work a sense of ownership for the vision. Everyone needs to believe they belong, can make a difference, bear accountability for their actions, and have a stake in the effort.

After surveying the walls and finalizing the strategy, Nehemiah appealed to the heads and hearts of the Jews. Their ancestors had been taken into exile, and they themselves had returned to Jerusalem only to become discouraged and ridiculed by the enemies surrounding them. As a result, Nehemiah convinced many of the city's residents to give up their livelihoods for a period of time to work on the wall. He brought together such unlikely professionals as goldsmiths, perfumers, and farmers to accomplish the feat. He did this by laying out a vision that captured their hearts and proposing a plausible strategy that engaged their minds for reaching this vision.

Vision energizes. It gets people off their chair, saying "yes" to the cause. Strategy captures the energy and channels it into concrete plans to achieve the vision. Aligning translates the hearts, minds, and resources of those energized by the vision into actions which implement the strategy and bring about the vision. When Nehemiah shared his vision and strategy, the people replied, "Let us start rebuilding." So Nehemiah divided them into forty-one teams, and they went to work on the wall.

ENCOURAGING

The journey from the present to our preferable future is always longer than first imagined, and it is almost always harder than most leaders and their followers anticipate. That is why the fourth Responsibility of a transformational leader, Encouraging, is so very crucial. The leader as encourager imparts courage and hope that keeps followers acting as owners on days when the going is unusually tough and renting is an attractive option.

The Encouraging leader helps those who have begun a vision-led journey to finish it by urging them on, by reminding them of their shared values and destiny, and by creating an environment in which they can encourage themselves.

Though aligned to Nehemiah's vision of a secure community, and having been presented a workable strategy, the builders panicked halfway through the project. "The workers are getting tired, and there is so much rubble to be moved. We will never be able to build the wall by ourselves," they cried. Fear took perhaps the greatest toll on the workers' strength. About the same time, local tribes threatened to attack the builders. Modifying his strategy, Nehemiah converted part of the workforce to a militia that stood between the builders and the threats from their enemies. He personally walked the perimeter, reminding them that God would fight for them and that their families were depending on them.

The builders all returned to their work on the wall, apparently with renewed vigor. Tuned into the emotional needs of his workers, Nehemiah had skillfully addressed and removed the distractions, divisions, and disturbances that stood between the workers and a finished wall. He had effectively engaged in the essential leadership Responsibility we call Encouraging.

Transformational Leaders Inspire:

Determination in people who are vacillating

Courage in people who are fearful

Action in people who are hesitating

Optimism in people who are cynical

Hope in people who are discouraged

Bring Your Best DICE + 1 to Each Responsibility

Earlier, we said the ability to effectively play each Role is directly related to a leader's **DICE + 1** capacity. In a similar manner, the ability to fulfill each essential Responsibility depends on the leader's **DICE + 1**.

Let's again consider the Responsibility of Vision-Casting. It takes an enormous amount of Dynamic Determination to cast a vision capable of transforming the lives of a leader and his followers. If the leader lacks Dynamic Determination—in other words, if he is not connected to a purpose larger than his own self-interest—it will be very difficult to cast a vision that will attract and inspire individuals to go the extra mile.

Similarly, Strategy-Making requires Intellectual Flexibility to see the world clearly and possess the courage to change one's mind based on what is observed. A leader with insufficient Intellectual Flexibility thinks rigidly that things can only be done one way. She will have a hard time recognizing opportunities and developing strategy to take advantage of those opportunities.

The same is true of Courageous Character and Emotional Maturity as they relate to the Responsibilities of Aligning and Encouraging. Anyone deficient in one of these virtue-based traits of consequence will find it hard to fulfill the essential Responsibilities of a transformational leader.

While we've linked one particular **DICE** trait with each Responsibility to show you how it works, remember that all traits of consequence represented by this acronym must be exercised together in order to successfully play each Role and Responsibility.

Digging Deeper into Vision-Casting

Let's consider how a business leader might engage in Vision-Casting across the playing fields of Roles. Playing the Role of Direction Setter, she might shape and share her vision for a purpose-driven culture focused on the customer her organization aspires to serve. In the Spokesperson's Role, that same leader might cast that same vision for a customer-friendly culture that connects those being served with the people and resources of the business. In the Coach's Role, she might shape and share her vision for a leadership-friendly culture that creates a pipeline to supply future leaders. Finally, in the Role of Change Agent, this leader might cast her vision for a learning culture that supports continuous, positive change within the organization. **Note:** *The vision is the same as she moves from one Role to another.*

The Vision-Casting process is about crafting and communicating a credible and emotionally satisfying future. As has been said, helping others see the future clearly and feel it deeply is the most important Responsibility of a transformational leader. Wise King Solomon recognized this truth. "Where there is no vision, the people perish," he wrote in the Book of Proverbs (KJV). The original language in which Proverbs was written suggests that energy scatters without vision. People go off in fifty different directions, and it's a waste of human effort when there is no foresight.

> Helping others see the future clearly and feel it deeply is the most important Responsibility of a leader.

In an organization where vision is lacking, the people in charge default to managing rather than leading. With no focused energy, these organizations often end up being dissolved or acquired because they have lost their way and, in the process, their competitive edge. The corporate graveyard is littered with the headstones of companies that had great management but poor leadership.

Take the Eastman Kodak Company, for instance. Founded in the late 1800s, this worldwide company employed 145,000 people at its peak, invented film photography, and sold this film through inexpensive cameras that almost everyone could afford. In 1976, the company made more than 90 percent of the film and 85 percent of the cameras sold in the U.S. But its leaders failed to cast a vision that included the technology the company itself had invented.

In 1975, a Kodak company engineer assembled the very first digital camera, but the company declined to develop the technology for fear of endangering its lucrative film business. Even when Apple employed Kodak to manufacturer one of the first digital cameras to be marketed, the venerable photographic company refused to switch its emphasis to digital photography. By the time it gave up on film cameras in 2004, it was too late. Eastman Kodak manufactured its last roll of film in 2009 and filed for Chapter 11 bankruptcy in 2012, its worldwide workforce reduced to just 18,000.

The energy of this once-proud organization had been scattered (some might say squandered) by leadership that stubbornly held onto short-term earnings instead of playing the Change Agent Role and casting a vision for

Kodak's participation in the digital revolution its own technology helped bring about.

Without vision, there really is no reason to sacrifice or take risks. There is no driving, compelling reason to change and begin doing new and uncomfortable things. In today's hyper-competitive environment, vision-poor companies get eaten alive by the vision-rich.

Apple is a prime example of a company that lost but then regained its vision. Steve Jobs and Steve Wozniak hatched Apple Computer in a garage in 1975, and in 1979 the company sold $200 million worth of computers. As the visionary, Jobs helped conceptualize and design a beginner-friendly personal computer. He brought to the masses the first color graphics and a keyboard (in the Apple II) and the first graphical-user interface controlled by a mouse (in the McIntosh).

While Job's vision launched Apple and kept it innovating, he lacked the skills to market, produce, and deliver what the company developed. For instance, Apple's unveiling of the McIntosh computer immediately created a year's worth of backorders. So Jobs hired John Sculley (PepsiCo's number two executive) to provide Apple's free-spirited "technology tinkerers" with some adult supervision and to help him run the business. Eventually, CEO Sculley pushed Jobs off the board of directors, and in 1985 Jobs left the very company he co-founded.

More than a decade later, Apple again found itself in desperate straits— this time from lack of vision. Facing intense competition, and having failed to develop the next-generation McIntosh operating system, Apple's share of the PC market had dropped to just 5.3 percent. Now a better-organized company, Apple had lost much of its culture of learning and adapting to change. In the early '90s it was on the brink of collapse.

Meanwhile Jobs had started NeXT computer. Although its sales were lackluster, NeXT developed technology that would be invaluable in future years. Plus, Jobs had purchased Pixar Animation Studios and guided it to dizzying success following Disney's release of Pixar's first feature-length, computer-animated film: *Toy Story*.

In 1996, Apple bought NeXT Computer and brought back a now more mature Steve Jobs to resuscitate the organization he helped start. Eventually, Apple put to use NeXT Computer's technology in the iPod, the iPhone, and the iPad, and its sales soared to previously unimaginable heights. As its CEO from 1997 to 2011, Jobs re-established the company's learning ethos, helped it regain vision, and lent it the considerable management skills he had accumulated while away.

CLOSING THOUGHTS ON VISION-CASTING

A life-giving vision that almost anyone can understand and that many will embrace has distinctive marks. We refer to these marks as the ABCDEFs of a transforming vision. Such a vision must be: Appropriate, Bold, Clear, Desirable, Energizing, and Feasible.

- *Appropriate:* A transforming vision "fits" the identity, culture, and history of those listening.

- *Bold:* A transforming vision is bold and breathtaking, not just in scope but in spirit and substance.

- *Clear:* A transforming vision makes things obvious and simple by focusing on a few critical things that can and must change if the world is to be a better place.

- *Desirable:* A transforming vision is inherently attractive, resonating deeply with the listeners' purpose and values.

- *Energizing:* Vision fires people up, transforming spectators into participants and renters into owners.

- *Feasible:* A transforming vision is

Steve Jobs was a brilliant visionary and strategist, but he made no claim to virtue. Although he transformed an industry, he was not an exemplary transformational leader. "He was not a model boss or human being, tidily packaged for emulation," says his authorized biographer, Walter Isaacson. "Driven by demons, he could drive those around him to fury and despair. But his personality and passions and products were all interrelated, just as Apple's hardware and software tended to be, as if part of an integrated system. His tale is thus both instructive and cautionary, filled with lessons about innovation, character, leadership, and values."

fiercely realistic and unflinchingly candid about the realities of the present and the difficulties likely to be encountered in moving forward.

All of a leader's essential Responsibilities are continuous, particularly Vision-Casting. She can't just cast a vision and say, "That's good enough. Now we'll start Strategy-Making or Aligning or Encouraging." Vision-Casting is not a linear, start-stop thing. It is part of an ongoing cycle that never stops.

Besides casting and shaping the vision, the transformational leader must talk about it constantly. "Effective information transfer almost always requires repetition," says Harvard professor John P. Kotter, advising that vision be communicated as often as possible, not just at formal meetings. Kotter contends that vision is typically under-communicated by a factor of 10.

Precisely because Vision-Casting is an on-going process, beware of buying into workshops where everyone sits around the table brainstorming ideas that are not feasible in the real world. The typical drill is to shoehorn these ideas into a statement that is then written on a piece of paper and posted on the wall of the meeting room. Thankfully, many of those so-called "vision statements" never see the light of day.

Rather than writing ideas down on bits of paper, the Vision-Casting we're talking about is done in the dust and sweat of real life, where a leader in touch with the present sees in his mind's eye a preferable future and communicates it to his followers face-to-face and heart-to-heart.

Boeing's Big Wager: A Case Study in Vision-Casting

When Boeing CEO Bill Allen decided to build the 707, he had no orders—he was building on spec. He simply believed customers would buy. It takes courage to bet the company's future on a vision.

At the beginning of the jet age, Boeing was a non-entity in the business of building commercial aircraft. They were pros at building military aircraft—bombers like the *B-17, B-52, B-47, B-36,* and the *KC135.* The *B-52* and *B-47* taught them how to build large jet aircraft.

But jets weren't commercially viable for airlines. To convert to jet technology would require a huge investment in technology and infrastructure that would play havoc with airlines' bottom lines. For Boeing, the safest choice would have been to stay in the military aviation sector, building world-class bombers. That, however, wasn't Allen's plan. He bet the company, so to speak, on a move to civil aviation in the form of one product.

Mr. Allen was convinced that consumers would love the comfort, speed and convenience of jet travel and that the civilian sector provided significantly more growth potential than the military sector. Allen was so sure of his conviction that he was willing to wager Boeing's financial future on it. In 1952 he persuaded Boeing's board of directors to invest in the 707, the first U.S. transatlantic commercial jetliner. That decision would change aviation and Boeing forever, but it was a big risk. All told, Boeing invested $185 million in the 707. According to a 1957 *Fortune* article, that was $36 million more than Boeing's net worth the previous year.

It was just one plane, but it remade a company, revolutionized an industry, and changed the world.

GAINING PERSONAL PERSPECTIVE

On August 28, 1963, Dr. Martin Luther King, Jr. delivered his now legendary "I Have a Dream" speech on the steps of the Lincoln Memorial to more than 200,000 civil rights demonstrators. To gain personal perspective on Vision-Casting, search online for the full text of the "I Have a Dream Speech" and reflect on how it illustrates the ABCDEFs of a transforming vision.

How does Dr. King's speech illustrate Vision-Casting in the following areas?

Appropriate

_____

_____

_____

Bold _____

_____

_____

Clear _____

_____

_____

Desirable _____

_____

_____

Energizing _____

_____

_____

Feasible _____

_____

_____

Strategy is About Choice

If a strategic statement does not tell the world what you will do and won't do, it is not a strategy. Strategy is about choice.

I (Jim) graduated from college during the Vietnam War and was drafted. I applied to enter Naval Aviation and eventually earned my wings, flying attack jets for five years on active duty and for another eight years in the Naval Reserves.

In the reserves, I flew an *A-3* attack jet that had been converted to an airborne tanker. One of our missions was to act as a pathfinder and tanker for flights of other attack jets or fighters moving from the West Coast to points in the Pacific. Usually, we would escort a flight of four *F-4* fighters, for example, from San Francisco to Hawaii.

Fuel considerations for these "TransPacs" were always critical. We had to have enough fuel to transfer to the planes we were escorting, and we had to have enough left for us to land safely. Therefore, it was extremely important to pick a route that would allow us to get to our destination safely.

Normally, we had three options from which to choose: a northern route, a southern route and a center route. We studied the weather, the high altitude winds, pressure, and temperatures to determine which route we would pick, the time we would depart, and the altitudes and speeds we would fly in order to maximize endurance.

The key was to pick one and stay with it. We could make adjustments along the way, but we would not have the fuel to change from, say, the northern route to the central route. We had to make a choice before departing, and that is a critical part of strategy.

It is easier to keep your options open but it is often fatal when it comes to determining strategy. You can't do all things. You must decide what you will do and will not do, and execute on the basis of those decisions.

6

Results of a Transformational Leader

The Ancient Text—The Book of Nehemiah 5:1-19

Nehemiah Defends the Oppressed

¹About this time some of the men and their wives raised a cry of protest against their fellow Jews. ²They were saying, "We have such large families. We need more food to survive."

³Others said, "We have mortgaged our fields, vineyards, and homes to get food during the famine."

⁴And others said, "We have had to borrow money on our fields and vineyards to pay our taxes. ⁵We belong to the same family as those who are wealthy, and our children are just like theirs. Yet we must sell our children into slavery just to get enough money to live. We have already sold some of our daughters, and we are helpless to do anything about it, for our fields and vineyards are already mortgaged to others."

⁶When I heard their complaints, I was very angry. ⁷After thinking it over, I spoke out against these nobles and officials. I told them, "You are hurting your own relatives by charging interest when they borrow money!" Then I called a public meeting to deal with the problem.

*8 At the meeting I said to them, "We are doing all we can to redeem our Jewish relatives who have had to sell themselves to pagan foreigners, but you are selling them back into slavery again. How often must we redeem them?" And they had nothing to say in their defense.

*9 Then I pressed further, "What you are doing is not right! Should you not walk in the fear of our God in order to avoid being mocked by enemy nations? 10 I myself, as well as my brothers and my workers, have been lending the people money and grain, but now let us stop this business of charging interest. 11 You must restore their fields, vineyards, olive groves, and homes to them this very day. And repay the interest you charged when you lent them money, grain, new wine, and olive oil."

12 They replied, "We will give back everything and demand nothing more from the people. We will do as you say." Then I called the priests and made the nobles and officials swear to do what they had promised.

13 I shook out the folds of my robe and said, "If you fail to keep your promise, may God shake you like this from your homes and from your property!"

The whole assembly responded, "Amen," and they praised the LORD. And the people did as they had promised.

14 For the entire twelve years that I was governor of Judah—from the twentieth year to the thirty-second year of the reign of King Artaxerxes—neither I nor my officials drew on our official food allowance. 15 The former governors, in contrast, had laid heavy burdens on the people, demanding a daily ration of food and wine, besides forty pieces of silver. Even their assistants took advantage of the people. But because I feared God, I did not act that way.

16 I also devoted myself to working on the wall and refused to acquire any land. And I required all my servants to spend time working on the wall. 17 I asked for nothing, even though I regularly fed 150 Jewish officials at my table, besides all the visitors from other lands! 18 The provisions I paid for each day included one ox, six choice sheep or goats, and a large number of poultry. And every ten days we needed a large supply of all kinds of wine. Yet I refused to claim the governor's food allowance because the people already carried a heavy burden.

19 Remember, O my God, all that I have done for these people, and bless me for it.

Nehemiah's Story Updated

Days passed and yet another crisis—this one internal—threatened to disrupt the repair of Jerusalem's walls.

Jotham worked next to farmers and common laborers who worked full-time on the wall. Ignoring their fields, the farmers had no grain to feed their families, and without a steady paycheck, the laborers had no money to pay taxes to the king. These fellow wall-builders were forced to borrow money to eat and pay taxes.

Wealthy Jews lent this money to their poorer neighbors, but they did so at 40% APR—the going rate in 445 BC. When loans could not be repaid, these opportunists began confiscating the land, animals and even children of those to whom they had advanced money. It was all legal, but it wasn't right, and cracks began to show in the morale of the wall-building crews, which consisted of both the "haves" and the "have-nots".

Jotham felt the tension and wondered what could prevent a wholesale riot. He didn't wonder for long. Because they had witnessed the integrity of Nehemiah in dealing with Jerusalem's outside enemies and in denying himself perks he could legally have claimed as governor, those workers drowning in debt found the courage to approach their leader.

When he learned what was going on, Nehemiah was livid, but before confronting the elites, he carefully considered his words. He started by reminding them of their shared responsibility, as God's people, to represent him well. "We've worked hard to free those who our enemies have enslaved," he said, reminding them of their shared goal to rebuild Jerusalem. "By placing a heavy burden on your fellow Jews, you're forcing them to sell their sons and daughters back into slavery." He added, "Think of what that says to our enemies about the character of the God we serve."

Nehemiah's argument hit home. No one spoke. They knew it was true.

"Now please," said the cupbearer-turned-governor, who could have issued an order rather than making a request, "...please, for the sake of the community whose integrity we are rebuilding, give your poorer cousins back their fields and houses and children, and make sure everyone has enough to live on while we finish repairing Jerusalem's walls." The affluent Jews swore they would repay all they had taken—and more.

Monitoring, Evaluating, and Responding to Outcomes

Uninterrupted progress is rare. This is especially true in the complex world in which we live. Even the best organizations move forward in fits and starts, occasionally taking one step forward and two steps back.

Bursts of enthusiasm, creativity, and new growth are often followed by stretches of mediocrity, wasted resources, and squandered opportunities. Hard-won ground is lost and hard-earned lessons forgotten.

Transformational leadership does not eliminate instances of poor performance, mistakes, or even outright failure, but it does provide for continual renewal and improvement by practicing a disciplined, collective approach to monitoring performance and constructively responding to feedback. This is the leadership work of Results. *See Figure 11.*

The Results ring of The 4-R Model represents outcomes that flow from the collective effort of leaders and followers participating in the four aspects of transformational leadership:

- *Relationships*–Drawing from a fund of personal virtue, **DICE +1**, to forge collaborative partnerships. *See Chapter 3.*

- *Roles*–Playing four essential parts that shape a mission-friendly, customer-friendly, leadership-friendly and learning-friendly culture. *See Chapter 4.*

- *Responsibilities*–Doing the actual work of leading. *See Chapter 5.*

- *Results*–Staying effective over time by monitoring performance and responding to feedback.

How to get important things accomplished isn't a great mystery, as General Electric CEO Jeff Immelt points out. "There is no real magic to being a leader," *Fast Company Magazine* quotes him as saying. "But at the end of the day, you have to spend your time around the things that are really important, like setting priorities, measuring outcomes, and rewarding them." That's what we'll cover in this chapter as we explain and then illustrate the Results of a Transformational Leader.

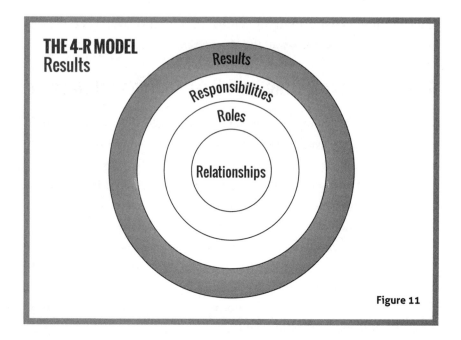

THE 4-R MODEL
Results

Results

Responsibilities

Roles

Relationships

Figure 11

RESULTS: A MORAL IMPERATIVE

First and foremost, Results is an exercise in stewardship which ultimately depends on the integrity of the leader. No matter the scope or complexity of the organization, a leader has been entrusted with things that don't belong to him. As such, a leader has a sacred obligation to leverage whatever he's been given—brand value, organizational reputation, finances, and talent—for the long-term welfare and progress of that trust.

As leadership consultant and author Peter Block puts it, "Stewardship asks us to serve our organizations and be accountable to them without caretaking and without taking control. And in letting caretaking and control go, we hold onto the spiritual meaning of stewardship: to honor what has been given to us, to use power with a sense of grace, and to pursue purposes that transcend short-term self-interest."

Our ancient friend Nehemiah had been entrusted by the king with the revitalization of the region's economy. He had also been entrusted by God with the restoration of the Jewish community in Jerusalem. As we learn in the final chapters of the ancient text, this cupbearer-turned-governor succeeded at both. Utilizing the resources and authority entrusted to him, he proved himself a "good steward" in the full sense of the phrase.

In stark contrast stands Dennis Kozlowski, former CEO of Tyco, the global security solutions and fire protection company. Kozlowski's technical-managerial expertise won him high praise from Wall Street and the company's shareholders. Tyco's revenues rose a remarkable 48.7% between 1997 and 2001, the same year *Business Week* pictured Kozlowski on their cover and hailed him as "The Most Aggressive CEO."

Unfortunately, Kozlowski let his successes go to his head. He blurred the line between company good and private gain. He came to believe that Tyco was his personal property. Kozlowski's excesses have been well publicized: a $6,000 shower curtain, a $15,000 doggie umbrella stand, and a $2 million birthday party for his wife on the island of Sardinia, disguised as a shareholder meeting so Tyco could pay half the bill.

Kozlowski closed out his leadership with a tangled mess of acquisitions, strategic errors, and self-indulgence. Charged with stealing $170 million directly from Tyco and fraudulently earning $430 million from the sale of stock, Koslowski and his CFO, Mark Schwartz, were convicted in federal court of grand larceny, conspiracy, falsifying records, and violating business law. Today, Kozlowski serves an 8½ to 25-year sentence at the Mid-State Correctional Facility in Marcy, New York where he earns one dollar a day cleaning floors and dishing food in the prison cafeteria.

Kozlowski made a colossal mess of things, not because he lacked knowledge or skill but out of a deficiency in character. He saw his authority as an inherent right, not a privilege. Ultimately, he proved a poor steward of his company.

Suppose you're a small l leader without a big budget like Nehemiah or Dennis Kozlowski. With what have you been entrusted? At a minimum you've been entrusted with your integrity and your good name. If you've been blessed with children, you've also been entrusted with their potential. Perhaps you lead a community non-profit with a tiny account but a handful of passionate volunteers. You may not lead thousands or have the time, talent, and treasure of others at your disposal. But you can potentially make the world right around you a better place by investing your own opportunities and gifting.

Being a good steward of whatever you've been entrusted forms the background against which we'll frame the Results aspect of transformational leadership.

CATEGORIES OF RESULTS

Results are the outcomes which flow from doing all you can to secure the welfare and progress of what you've been entrusted. Every time a leader interacts with those outside or inside an organization, there is an outcome.

These outcomes fall into two categories: Quantitative Results and Qualitative Results. Nehemiah witnessed both. The Quantitative Result of his leadership was that the walls were repaired in a short time span. The Qualitative Result was that, over fifty-two days, forty-one teams of very diverse people figured out how to work together toward shared goals and values. In the process, they regained their identity as a community of God's chosen people.

In a major corporation, new strategies may produce Quantitative Results like quarterly sales increases or Qualitative Results like consumers taking ownership of a brand they trust—hence insider clubs like My Verizon or My Panera Bread.

As a result of a leader's efforts to align its non-paid staff to its vision, a community action group may log more volunteer hours (Quantitative) or new members may feel more welcomed (Qualitative).

Leaders must deliver Results. That is non-negotiable. Results may not come on a timetable, despite a leader's wise investment in the time, talent, and treasure. But when they have done their best with what they have been entrusted, results will eventually come.

Let's take another look at Nehemiah's example. While breaches in the city walls were being mended (positive Quantitative Results), cracks were growing in the unity of the community of builders (negative Qualitative Results). Because they spent all their time on this urgent community project, the laborers had no time to work at their own day-to-day occupations. Wealthy Jews extracted heavy penalties from Jews with less means who were forced to borrow to eat and pay taxes during the special wall-building effort. Animosity between the two sides threatened to undermine their mutual goals of repairing Jerusalem's wall and revitalizing their standing as God's chosen people.

You might say the city's reconstruction/reunification effort experienced what wise leaders today refer to as "vision leak." Vision-Casting, as the grammar suggests, is a process rather than an event. It is insufficient to communicate vision only once. It must be constantly reinforced, clarified, updated as necessary, and kept at the forefront of daily organizational life. In Nehemiah's case, the entire community took their eyes off the prize as well-to-do Jews reaped short-time profits and their poorer cousins worried about their next meal.

Informed of this unintended outcome, Nehemiah invested his reputation for straight talk and personal integrity in a potentially volatile confrontation with the upper crust.

Nehemiah knew what the money lenders were doing was technically legal but morally wrong. He himself had lent money, but not at exorbitant rates. Moreover, Nehemiah knew that God had prohibited his people from laying a heavy financial burden on their fellow Jews and on enslaving them. So, rather than exercise his power as governor, and twist the law to his advantage, Nehemiah appealed to the hearts of the money lenders and the values they shared.

He recast the vision for a unified community and realigned them with the priorities of securing Jerusalem and making God look good in the eyes of its neighbors. In doing this, Nehemiah achieved positive Qualitative Results by defusing the crisis and bringing the community back together. Quantitative Results followed as work on the wall resumed.

It's notable that, in order to sustain Quantitative outcomes, a leader must pay attention to the Qualitative outcomes like morale, teamwork, collaboration, and inspiration. It's a both/and proposition.

> In order to sustain Quantitative outcomes, a leader must pay attention to the Qualitative outcomes like morale, teamwork, collaboration, and inspiration.

MEASURING RESULTS

Results are not only about outcomes. Both little **l** or big **L** leaders must be clear about what they want to happen as a consequence of their leadership efforts, so they can monitor and measure how they doing and make adjustments that will produce even better results. Receiving and analyzing feedback and making course corrections is all part of the Results aspect of transformational leadership. That said, the most important things in life are typically the hardest to measure and these are usually qualitative.

In Chapter 4, Nehemiah paid close attention to critical outcomes of the construction project that his vision-casing had set in motion. He observed that the wall had been built to half its height, but he was also told by reliable sources, and perhaps he could see it himself, that the strength of the laborers was failing. Moreover, the Jews' enemies had threatened to attack the laborers. Despite the Quantitative Results achieved in the early days of construction, the entire effort was in danger of collapsing. So Nehemiah made adjustments to his original strategy and organization of the work, to protect the laborers against attack. He also realigned and encouraged the laborers by reminding them of their common values and vision to rebuild not only the walls but also the community of Jerusalem as a part of God's promise to bring his people home. This encouraged the hearts of the workers (a Qualitative Result) and work on the wall continued (a Quantitative Result).

MAKING ADJUSTMENTS

A critical component of Results is measuring outcomes. A leader can't improve unless he pays attention to outcomes. If outcomes don't match what the leader expects, he has an opportunity to diagnose the problem.

As we read in Chapter 4 of the ancient text, Nehemiah took both Quantitative and Qualitative measurements of the outcomes to his leadership of the wall-building effort. Quantitatively, work on the wall had stalled. Qualitatively, morale had plummeted.

Results flow from the collective effort of leaders and followers participating in the Responsibilities, Roles and Relationships. What can a transformational leader do when she observes outcomes that don't meet expectations? For one thing, she can ask: "Have I done all I can to secure the welfare and progress of what I've been entrusted?" Here's where The 4-R Model can help in diagnosing the problem by working backwards from the Results component of the model. Ask yourself:

• *Am I engaging in the Responsibilities of a leader?*

- *Am I playing the Roles of a leader?*

- *Do I have the sufficient* **DICE + 1** *to enter into and maintain collaborative Relationships? In some cases, Results may fall short because people doing the work have lost respect for their leaders.*

If he were alive today, Nehemiah would only need to look back to the Responsibilities of a transformational leader to find out why the work on the wall had stalled. The people had clearly lost vision through a combination of backbreaking work and the constant threat of attack.

Nehemiah met this challenge by adjusting Strategy and Encouraging the workers. He divided his workforce between building the wall and defending the builders. Nehemiah personally stood guard against enemy attack, and he appealed to the workers' shared faith. "Our God will fight for us," he declared.

Four Principles for Improving Results

There are numerous ways to measure outcomes. Whether you lead a business, a non-profit, a governmental institution, or a family, pay attention to these four principles:

1. *Be Clear About Intended Results*–Ask: "What outcomes are critical to the fulfillment of my organization's mission, vision, and values?"

2. *Measure What Matters*–Ask: "What measurements would be most meaningful in determining whether we are getting those outcomes?"

3. *Look for Meaning in the Outcomes*–Ask: "Why are we not getting the results we want? Is it due to failure in my relationships, roles, or responsibilities—or things beyond my control?"

4. *Make Adjustments*–Considering the gap between expected and actual outcomes, and based on your analysis of the reasons for this gap, ask: "What changes should I make in my leadership?"

In the process of measuring Results, avoid the pitfalls of measuring nothing or measuring too much. Some people go through life thinking everything will take care of itself. They never get clear on what matters, and they fail to measure critical outcomes.

That's one extreme. The other extreme, often the case in business, is to measure everything simply because they can. Evaluating too much can complicate the picture and make it hard to determine which Results deserve the most attention.

A good rule of thumb is to measure only those key performance indicators that reveal whether you and your organization are making progress in light of your mission.

Listen to the Customer

The importance of good feedback cannot be overestimated. There are plenty of examples where lack of feedback, or inattention to good feedback, produced disastrous results.

One such instance is the astonishing length of time it took for pharmaceutical manufacturer Merck to withdraw its new pain reliever, Vioxx, from the market in 2004. This, despite mounting external and internal feedback that the drug was harming its users.

"In 2001, Merck's own report to federal regulators showed that 14.6% of Vioxx patients suffered from cardiovascular troubles while taking the drug and 2.5% developed serious problems, including heart attacks," reports the *Harvard Business Review*. The year before, a *New England Journal of Medicine* article had claimed patients taking Vioxx, rather than the alternative drug naproxen, were four times more likely to have a heart attack.

While indications have surfaced that Merck's sales representatives misled the medical community, even physicians who read the medical journal article may have discounted the alarm bells sounding, since many of their patients were offering anecdotal praise for the effectiveness of the new pain killer.

On the other hand, reliable feedback from those serving and those being served by a leader or organization can rescue a floundering enterprise (like the rebuilding of the Jerusalem wall) or make a good enterprise even better.

> A good rule of thumb is to measure only those key performance indicators that reveal whether your organization is making progress in light of its mission.

Buffalo Wild Wings, also known as B-Dubs, offers a window into the use of reliable feedback to achieve even greater heights.

Known for their excellent finger food and multi-screen sports entertainment in a fun, upbeat environment, this Minneapolis-based company had already achieved *Forbes Magazine's* 200 Best Small Companies list for five years when it embarked on an ambitious quest: to find out what was most important to attracting and retaining their core consumers.

Sources close to the company tell us that B-Dubs employed surveys and other statistical instruments to assess many components of their brand, including restaurant lay-out, décor, menu, hours, wait staff, and so forth. What they found—what mattered most to their core customers and kept them coming back—was the continuity of the wait staff.

It was as simple as their consumers getting to know the wait staff, and the wait staff getting to know them. B-Dubs locations with staff longevity exhibited an almost Cheers-like environment. Armed with this information, the company doubled down on finding ways to retain their wait staff. This stands as a good example of using data to understand what really matters, and then leveraging that knowledge to continually improve Results.

Good feedback is absolutely important if companies want to improve their products or leaders want to improve their leadership ability. It is difficult to improve without reliable input from the customers or followers they served. The same applies to leading a family. Without feedback from a spouse or children, progress will falter.

Earl Weaver, terror of American League umpires over sixteen years as manager of the Baltimore Orioles, was known for his epic rants. Weaver once stormed onto the field to argue a call, screaming to the umpire, "Are you going to get any better, or is this it?"

This is the fundamental question for any leader or organization striving for effectiveness in the twenty-first century. Are we going to get any better? Will

Cheers was a television sitcom staged in a Boston, Massachusetts bar of the same name. Everyday people gathered to socialize at this neighborhood watering hole where, as the theme-song states, "everybody knows your name."

we come to terms with the issues involved in poor performance, self-correct, learn new behaviors, and do whatever is necessary to stay effective? Or is this it? Is this as good as we'll ever get?

GAINING PERSONAL PERSPECTIVE

How are you doing in your leadership role? Individual leaders and organizations need a performance base line—a set of reference points to interpret good feedback.

Past Performance–How are you doing compared to last year or last month? Are you improving or getting worse?

_____

_____

_____

Peer Performance–How are you doing compared to others in a similar situation, industry, or work context? Are you out-performing or under-performing them?

_____

_____

_____

Future Performance–How are you doing in light of critical outcomes that must be achieved next month or next year to support your purpose, vision, and values?

_____

_____

_____

Seven Practical Ideas

Consider these common-sense solutions that Results-oriented leaders can apply now.

1. *Outcomes Not Activities*—Refine your performance goals and objectives to describe critical outcomes your organization needs to achieve versus activities and busyness which may or may not produce needed results.

2. *Assess Current Results*—Perform an honest assessment of the current Result level you are achieving and identify the gap between what is desired and what you are delivering.

3. *Own the Results*—Take personal responsibility for Results and be transparent in your motivation to achieve positive Results. Make sure it isn't a selfish play for personal gain but has the interest of your organization at heart.

4. *Communicate Expectations*—Clearly and specifically communicate performance expectations to your team members. Be sure they see the outcomes, not just the activities.

> **This list of Seven Practical Ideas is modified from ideas presented by Dave Ulrich, Jack Zenger, and Norm Smallwood in *Results-Based Leadership*.**

5. *Provide Standards and Metrics*—Identify the numbers you need to assess how you and your team are doing. If necessary, spend time defining clear metrics that indicate whether desired outcomes are being achieved.

6. *Innovate*—Be experimental and innovate to find new ways of improving performance. The best leaders are open to new and better ways of getting Results.

7. *Bias for Action*—Always be looking to take action. Pausing and being strategic is important, but the best Results-based leaders lean into action.

Virtue and Today's Leader

The Ancient Text—The Book of Nehemiah

Selected Text Relating to the Rebuilding of the Wall and the Community

Nehemiah 6:15-16

[15] *So on October 2 the wall was finished—just fifty-two days after we had begun.* [16] *When our enemies and the surrounding nations heard about it, they were frightened and humiliated. They realized this work had been done with the help of our God.*

Nehemiah 7:1-3

[1] *After the wall was finished and I had set up the doors in the gates, the gate-keepers, singers, and Levites were appointed.* [2] *I gave the responsibility of governing Jerusalem to my brother Hanani, along with Hananiah, the commander of the fortress, for he was a faithful man who feared God more than most.* [3] *I said to them, "Do not leave the gates open during the hottest part of the day. And even while the gatekeepers are on duty, have them shut and bar the doors. Appoint the residents of Jerusalem to act as guards, everyone on a regular watch. Some will serve at sentry posts and some in front of their own homes."*

Nehemiah 8:1-3

¹ All the people assembled with a unified purpose at the square just inside the Water Gate. They asked Ezra the scribe to bring out the Book of the Law of Moses, which the Lord had given for Israel to obey.

² So on October 8, Ezra the priest brought the Book of the Law before the assembly, which included the men and women and all the children old enough to understand. ³ He faced the square just inside the Water Gate from early morning until noon and read aloud to everyone who could understand. All the people listened closely to the Book of the Law.

Nehemiah 11: 1-2

¹ The leaders of the people were living in Jerusalem, the holy city. A tenth of the people from the other towns of Judah and Benjamin were chosen by sacred lots to live there, too, while the rest stayed where they were. ² And the people commended everyone who volunteered to resettle in Jerusalem.

Nehemiah 12:27-29

²⁷ For the dedication of the new wall of Jerusalem, the Levites throughout the land were asked to come to Jerusalem to assist in the ceremonies. They were to take part in the joyous occasion with their songs of thanksgiving and with the music of cymbals, harps, and lyres. ²⁸ The singers were brought together from the region around Jerusalem and from the villages of the Netophathites.

²⁹ They also came from Beth-gilgal and the rural areas near Geba and Azmaveth, for the singers had built their own settlements around Jerusalem.

Authors' Note: As you have time and opportunity, the authors of this book recommend reading the entire ancient text of Nehemiah 6:1–13:30.

Nehemiah's Story Updated

Jotham was thrilled to be heading home. The walls of Jerusalem had been restored in an amazing fifty-two days. Behind these walls, hopes soared. The Jews resettled the city, and Nehemiah appointed key municipal leaders. None held jobs as important as those who opened the city's heavy wooden gates each morning and closed them every evening. Merchants gained confidence that their goods would be protected against attack. Commerce returned, and the city thrived. Taxes from this commerce flowed to Susa as King Artaxerxes expected when he sent Nehemiah on his 900-mile journey.

Something even more amazing happened in the hearts of the people. Having watched their God protect and provide as they rebuilt the walls, the Jews were now ready to renew their covenant with Him. Soon after construction finished, a priest named Ezra began publicly reading from their Holy Book. All the Jews stood at attention and for the first time in many years they took God's word seriously. "We agree," they declared.

At the wall's dedication, the people celebrated not only the rebuilding of a physical barrier protecting them from outside enemies but their internal reconnection as God's chosen people. No longer would they be viewed as a conquered nation to be exploited. No longer were they ashamed of their heritage. The walls, and also the hearts of the people, had been secured. This was what Nehemiah hoped and prayed for when he boldly faced the king and later a sad-faced crowd in Jerusalem soon after arriving in 445 BC.

Now, twelve years later, the cupbearer-turned-governor had been recalled to Susa. His friend Jotham would return with him. The court reporter had changed. He had grown in character and commitment. Besides recording the rebuilding of the wall, as the king had instructed, he had personally participated in the historic event. As he applied each layer of mortar and helped lift large stones into the gaps, Jotham came to own this project and embrace its potential for making Jerusalem whole. At the end of each day, he wrote down not only how many feet the wall had risen but also the life-changing stories of very diverse people who had joined hands to create a better life for all.

Jotham himself had been transformed into a leader: proposing to his fellow workers what could be done each day, outlining a way to achieve those goals, rallying his team to each task, and encouraging them in difficult circumstances. Despite his upbringing in distant Susa, Jotham had become a friend they could trust, and many followed his example—becoming leaders themselves.

Securing the last of his belongings, Jotham swung onto his mount and nudged it ahead, through the city gate. Transformed by the power of a higher noble purpose, he would never be the same. *"What else could I do to make a difference?"* Jotham wondered, as he rode down the path toward his next adventure.

The New Normal World

Like Nehemiah and Jotham, twenty-first century leaders and followers struggle to address difficulties ranging from global economic instability and the threat of terrorism to fractured companies, communities, and families. Because so much has changed in such a short period of time, the way we did things fifty, or even twenty, years ago won't produce the same Results today.

The term The New Normal was coined by investment industry visionary Roger McNamee in 2004 to describe the newest state of affairs in which we find ourselves during the opening decades of a new century. It is used to describe a series of social, economic, and political sea changes which have together created a new social landscape full of disruptive threats, sporadic change, and stomach-turning twists and turns. What was once the exception is now a new version of normal.

It is impossible to pinpoint an exact date when The New Normal began, but the most likely candidate is March 10, 2000, when the NASDAQ began its sharp decline from historic highs. Since then, we have lived in an age of uncertainty and disruptive change filled with terrorism, failed leaders and institutions, economic roiling, and geo-political instability.

What happened at 1:45 p.m. CDT (2:45 EDT) on May 6, 2010, aptly illustrates The New Normal. I (Mark) was beginning an afternoon teaching session when a student raised his hand and said we had better take a look at our favorite Internet news site. In a flash crash, the Dow had dropped a gut-wrenching 1,014.14 points (over 7%) in a fifteen minute period, and then almost immediately rebounded. It was the second-largest point swing and the biggest one-day point decline on an intraday basis in Dow Jones history. One trillion dollars in market value had temporarily disappeared. Procter & Gamble stock dropped nearly 37% before rebounding within minutes to its original levels.

Other cataclysmic global events include:

Sept. 11, 2001–The terrorist attack on the World Trade Towers and the Pentagon which revealed a new kind of warfare that has raged globally ever since.

Dec. 26, 2004–The Indian Ocean earthquake and the resulting tsunami killing almost 250,000 people in fourteen countries.

Fall of 2008–The beginning of an economic downturn from which the world has yet to fully recover.

March 11, 2011–A massive earthquake in Japan which shifted part of the landscape by as much as thirteen feet and triggered a tsunami killing over 150,000. This localized catastrophe disrupted economic activities around the globe.

LIVING WITH UNCERTAINTY

The U.S. Army created a framework for understanding The New Normal at its War College in Carlisle, Pennsylvania in the early 1990s to help officers get a handle on the dynamic cultural, technological, and geo-political forces shaping the world after the Soviet Union collapsed. This framework is described by the acrostic **VUCA**, which stands for Volatile, Uncertain, Complex, and Ambiguous.

Volatile describes something that is quick to vaporize or disappear—something difficult to capture or hold permanently. In The New Normal, the forces of globalization, geopolitical instability, and hyper-competition have conspired to fuel sporadic change at levels never before witnessed. Today, we live with continuous gyrations in the price of gasoline and precipitous drops or advances in the Dow, rather than the minimal adjustments of the past. Volatility is embedded in the fabric of our world and manifested in disruptive changes occurring throughout our most cherished institutions—from business and government to church and family.

Uncertain conjures images of something in flux, irregular and indefinite. The New Normal world is dimly lit. Surprises lurk in the shadows. The impact of change and the problems associated with it are so confusing, vague, and imprecise as to make solutions nothing more than educated guesswork. Little is clear. Final proof is rare. Nothing is conclusive. The future is less and less an extension of what has happened in the past. In The New Normal, we face an unpredictable world in a constant state of imbalance, and we waver in a chronic state of indecision.

Complex speaks to the interweaving and entangling of many strands. The shifting, roiling New Normal landscape is the product of a dense, interwoven overlay of constantly interacting economic, social, political, and cultural factors producing a dynamic situation impossible to understand, let alone control or predict.

Ambiguous is an adjective suggesting two or more possible meanings or interpretations of the same facts. In a complex New Normal world lacking clear-cut cause-and-effect sequences, there is often more than one reasonable way to see things or to make sense of a situation. The flow of events is puzzling; the facts may be vague and misleading. It becomes difficult to choose sound priorities, and we find ourselves busy but unproductive and without direction.

NEHEMIAH IN THE REAR-VIEW MIRROR

VUCA also describes the ancient world in which Nehemiah lived and led. Certainly there was ambiguity in the political situation which greeted the new governor upon his arrival in Jerusalem, as well as uncertainty and insecurity with the broken-down walls. The complexity of interactions between the king, the local tribes, the nobles, and the average Jewish citizens made it difficult to predict what would happen. The work of rebuilding the wall was accomplished in an environment of political, military, and emotional volatility that swung wildly from elation, as the wall progressed, to despair, as enemies threatened.

Nehemiah's virtue-driven leadership proved effective in this dynamic environment. His character won him the trust of the king who had stopped the rebuilding of the wall just fourteen years earlier. His character won the hearts of the Jews who signed onto his vision despite fierce opposition by their neighbors. His character kept him cool as he dealt with external threats of violence and internal threats of civil unrest. Character mattered in Nehemiah's day, and character still counts.

Nehemiah's leadership was driven by a passion for a purpose higher than himself. The 4-R Model calls this Dynamic Determination. He possessed the ability to see himself and others clearly, and the moral strength to change his attitude and behavior to match what he was seeing. The 4-R Model calls this Intellectual Flexibility. He had the moral integrity and courage necessary to earn the trust of those he led. The 4-R Model calls this Courageous Character. Finally, Nehemiah possessed a high degree of

Emotional Maturity which allowed him to remain steady under pressure and exercise a calming effect on his anxious and discouraged followers.

As a result of his virtuous character, Nehemiah was able to develop collaborative Relationships, both with the king and with various elements of Jewish population. Had The 4-R Model been around 2,500 years ago, we would have said Nehemiah had a high **DICE + 1** capacity. This ability to partner-up with all kinds of people allowed him to play the Roles and fulfill the Responsibilities necessary to see Results like the walls of Jerusalem being rebuilt in fifty-two days. But these Results began with Nehemiah's Relationships, which depended on his virtue—the center of the model and the starting point for anyone who would lead transformationally.

A rebuilt and restored Jerusalem had been predicted in the ancient Hebrew writings. But a catalyst was needed—someone to ignite the spark that turned this vision into reality. Nehemiah served as that catalyst. Every transformational leader acts as a catalyst to turn vision into reality.

Everyone Can Make a Difference

While few of us will occupy a position like Nehemiah, with a significant platform and outcomes of historic proportion, all of us are called to make a difference where we are. *Anyone with relationships has a platform.* It might be your family, your sports team, or your division at work, but we encourage you to consider your platform—the people that may be influenced through your interactions with them.

Most of us have no idea how we will impact others. As we move through life, we can be catalysts and set in motion things that will produce chain reactions beyond anything we can imagine. We simply do not know the ripple effect or the number of people who may be touched by our leadership.

Everyone has access to the virtue required to lead, although not everyone will work to develop the **DICE + 1** capacity we've described in this book. That's because growing in virtue is difficult. We liken it to preparing for a sporting event by running wind sprints or lifting weights. It is a rigorous process and takes commitment. But just as anyone who is motivated to run a marathon can do so by training, so anyone who wants to learn, grow, and develop virtue can do so.

Are you motivated to do what it takes to be a good husband or wife? The same holds true for being a good mother or father, a good team leader, or a leader of an organization. Whether a big **L** or little **l**, you must be exceptionally motivated to acquire the virtue necessary to lead well in any of the above situations. The demands upon you will be extraordinary, and they will not let up.

VIRTUE CAN BE LEARNED

Whatever we believe about our relationship with God, we can all align with a noble purpose beyond our self-interest. We can all grow in our wisdom to navigate life's difficult situations. We can all develop maturity by learning how to recognize and regulate our emotional life and by taking responsibility for the outcomes of our actions.

You'll find you have traction and that you can indeed make progress if you have four things in place: Motivation, Experience, Exemplars and Feedback.

Motivation—You must conclude that reality demands virtue of all who aspire to a good life and effective leadership. Virtue names the moral requirements minimally needed for a viable society, community, or organization. The seven cardinal virtues discussed in Chapters 3 and 4 and represented by the **DICE** traits of consequence must be displayed at sufficient levels for a leader to establish collaborative relationships. That's **DICE + 1**. Developing virtue is a rigorous process that takes commitment. Anyone who aspires to this process must be convinced of their need to develop virtue.

Experience—Virtue must be practiced by giving it a try and being willing to make improvements. You must be open to the possibility that sooner or later you will come face-to-face with your shortcomings. To pursue virtue is not the same as achieving perfection. Rather, it means committing yourself to a rigorous developmental process that asks you to face the demands of reality, identify the gaps in your capacity to meet these demands, and take steps to fill the gaps. It is not a destination. It is a life-long journey.

Exemplars—You need inspiring examples that manifest a particular virtue to a high degree. Use discretion in choosing these models. They are not saints. Even Mother Theresa struggled with doubt. They are flesh and blood human beings who wrestled in various ways with virtue gaps, human frailty, and insecurities. Nevertheless, they lived and led well. Virtue set their course, lit their path, and paved their way. Their shining examples call us to stay in the process and up our game.

Feedback—You cannot live a virtuous life alone; you need others. You are not made a virtuous person in isolation. Rather, virtue is developed in a social context. We all need the help and encouragement of trusted friends and mentors to sustain our journey toward the virtuous life. Aristotle compared the acquisition of virtue to learning to play an instrument. It requires not only dedication and practice, but also a teacher who knows how to play and gives constructive feedback.

ORDINARY PEOPLE IN ORDINARY TIMES

In this book, we've shared great moments in history when some now-famous people led well. We are not suggesting, though, that transformational leadership takes place only in the great moments. Far from it. Most leadership occurs in the small moments and prepares us for any great moments that may come our way.

The rescuers of World War II (profiled in Chapter 3) got in the habit of doing good so that, when the great moment came and a Jewish family knocked on their doors at 3 a.m., they could do nothing else. Later research indicated that those who gave sanctuary had been preparing for this all their lives by doing ordinary acts of kindness like bringing books to shut-ins, feeding stray animals, and so forth.

That's a powerful lesson. We all need to get ready. Every day is the raw material of the future. Every day offers an opportunity for actions and interactions that will either prepare us for what's next or make us less capable of responding. As American clergyman Philip Brooks said, "Character may be manifested in the great moments, but it is made in the small ones."

Nor are we born into leadership, as the Great Man Theory would have us believe. Leadership is not the province of an elite few who exhibit extraordinary characteristics like charisma or hyper-competency. That's a widely propagated myth.

Rather, leadership is about ordinary people in ordinary moments acting in a way that is constructive and serving the interests of others. This can happen in a single conversation with a friend or neighbor, or it can happen around the dinner table at home. No matter where you exercise leadership, virtue gives you maximum influence in that platform, and it sets in motion a chain reaction of moral influence far beyond your expectations.

> Every day is the raw material of the future.

Sometimes leadership calls you to control your reactions to stressful and demanding situations. This starts by choosing to monitor and regulate your emotional life.

Again, we're not talking about great moments on a world class platform, but about ordinary people in the ordinary interactions of life choosing, often at great personal sacrifice and risk, to act in a virtuous way. You might not be a Spokesperson on a large stage, but you will find yourself in a position to represent the interests of your team or your family to others on the outside.

The 4-R model can be superimposed over any interaction or setting—a family, a church, a non-profit organization, or a business enterprise.

Are You Ready to Lead?

So, what are you passionate about?

Passion is basically a higher purpose come to roost in your life that energizes you to take extraordinary, even sacrificial action. Nehemiah was minding his own business when a momentous opportunity came his way. He had a great job as cupbearer to the king and was, by all accounts, living a satisfying life. Then the report came from Jerusalem that deeply moved him.

So, what deeply bothers or concerns you in a constructive way— enough to take action to address the problem? Are there others who identify with your growing discontentment?

When Nehemiah arrived in Jerusalem, he found its residents just going through the motions. After assessing the situation, the new governor met with those who would do the work. "Do you see that?" he might have asked, pointing to the city's broken-down walls and fire-blackened gates. "Let me remind you that this should bother you, enough to take action."

Then he said, "Come, let us rebuild..." The people looked beyond their own self-interests and took responsibility for a public problem. "Let us start rebuilding," they said. Nehemiah's constructive proposal aroused the people and directed a stream of energy at the task before them.

Are you ready to lead like Nehemiah? As a way of answering this question, complete the following questions.

GAINING PERSONAL PERSPECTIVE

What higher purpose beyond your self-interest are you willing to go all out for?

_____

_____

_____

Define your passion. What are you willing to sacrifice for? What bothers you in a good way?

_____

_____

_____

Have you identified others that are similarly concerned? Can you clearly articulate your concern and why others ought to be involved?

_____

_____

_____

Can you list three constructive steps to start addressing this concern?

_____

_____

_____

Epilogue:
Two Present-Day
Transformational Leaders

Since retiring from Procter & Gamble in 2004, I (Jim) have had the privilege of traveling to the continent of Africa regularly to work with an African-based organization focused on reducing poverty through helping individuals establish their own businesses.

Like some Americans at the top of their companies, organizations, or families, many African leaders selfishly cling to power, refusing to give responsibility and opportunity to promising followers for fear those followers may someday replace them. As a result, Africa suffers from a severe shortage in its leadership pipeline.

During my travels, however, I have met two transformational leaders that would put many of America's best to shame. Allow me to briefly tell their stories.

Andrew Cunningham: Helping Others Reach Their Potential

A tall, rugged Caucasian with blondish-brown hair, Andrew is a gregarious outdoorsman. He talks with a South African accent, wears hats resembling Crocodile Dundee, and is fond of driving beat up old trucks.

A third-generation Zimbabwean, Andrew was one of four children born to David and Janet Cunningham. Their neighbors loved the Cunninghams.

After finishing school in Zimbabwe, Andrew attended university in Edinburgh, UK where he met his wife Claire. Shortly after marrying, Andrew and Claire moved to Mozambique, during that country's civil war, to work with a local church doing agricultural training and supplying food to a local hospital. Here Andrew got very sick with malaria and dysentery leading to an immune system collapse and ten years of severe weakness.

Andrew and Claire moved from Mozambique with their small daughter Zoe to Zimbabwe for rest and recuperation. His illness had a profound impact on Andrew's outlook. He came to deeply understand and value the reality of Jesus' words to the Apostle Paul in his second letter to the Corinthians: "My grace is sufficient for you, for my power is made perfect in weakness."

One day, sitting on a high rock overlooking a huge vista of dry bush, Andrew concluded that his purpose and calling was to help others reach their fullest potential, to become all that God created them to be. This influenced his approach to family, business and community, and led to a passionate desire to be part of an empowering environment where others could grow.

Andrew joined his brother, Peter, in the ostrich and poultry business he had started on the family ranch. Peter's emphasis on business and Andrew's heart for development, with their combined passion to do all things for the glory of God, led to a unique business model. The Cunninghams linked their feed mill, hatchery, and a world-class meat processing and tanning facility with small-scale farmers who produced the ostriches and chickens on a contract basis. As the business grew, they looked for more ways to engage with and be part of developing their community. For example, they founded a private school known as Ebenezer. This school offers an education and a future to the poorest of the poor. Students attending this school are each given a hectare of land to farm for two years. In the morning, they study scripture and agriculture. In the afternoon they work their land, growing chickens, cabbages, lettuce, carrots, and a variety of other crops. The students sell whatever they harvest and keep the money. At the end of two years, most have a stake of $3,000-$4,000 with which to go back to their villages and set up their own farms. There is only one requirement—each has agreed to teach people in their village how to farm.

Early in the twenty-first century, the government of their home country embarked on a controversial program of land distribution and began seizing white-owned farming operations. The Cunninghams agreed to diversify. Peter continued to farm in Zimbabwe while Andrew, his wife Claire and their two children moved to central Mozambique. There they started from scratch (on a dirt road with no electricity and the family living in tents) to build an integrated poultry operation: New Horizons Mozambique Lda.

The Cunninghams contract with hundreds of Mozambicans who grow out the birds. The birds are processed through a state-of-the-art facility, providing top quality frozen poultry meat throughout Mozambique.

As New Horizons has flourished, so has the surrounding area. The concept of "Communities of Fusion" has emerged, bringing together other entities and individuals with diverse skills and emphasis, but with a common purpose:

- Following the success of the broiler chicken model, two commercial egg operations have been established in the local community.

- A private academic school taking students to university entrance level has just completed its second year.

- A Mozambican Ebenezer College, similar to the school in Zimbabwe, has just opened with its first students.

- A growing work within local churches, which emphasizes primary health, is having a grass roots effect in the community.

New Horizon's poultry operations and other initiatives attract top talent from across Africa and Europe who want to come to work there—not because of what they get out of it materially, but because they know they are part of something much bigger than themselves.

As for his personal motivation, Andrew told me, "You know, the whole deal here is not about business; it's about showing God's love to people, because everything we have is his."

Sammy Gumbe: Man with Unstoppable Purpose

Born to a Mozambican ambassador and his wife, Sammy spent most of his early life in Kenya. He was a tall, imposing man, in good physical shape but very outgoing and fun loving. After completing school in Kenya, Sammy continued his education at a university in the United Kingdom. Returning to Kenya, he joined Standard Bank in Nairobi and began a promising career with this solid financial institution.

Following his conversion to Christianity, Sammy left his position with Standard Bank (to the distress of his father and mother) and enrolled in a Bible school. Upon graduating from the Bible School in 2000, Sammy and his wife Christine moved to the capital city of Maputo in his home country of Mozambique, with the intent of training pastors and church leaders.

The need was great. During Mozambique's 1977-1992 civil war, approximately 1.5 million refugees sought asylum in neighboring Malawi, Zimbabwe, Swaziland, Zambia, Tanzania, and South Africa. While in those countries, many refugees had confessed Christianity. After the war, they returned to Mozambique and wanted to start churches, but their pastors had little or no formal education.

Sammy saw the need to educate pastors and that was what he poured his energy into doing.

When Sammy and Christine exited the South African Airlines plane at Maputo January 19, 2001, they had exactly $391 and the clothes in their suitcase. They had no supporting organization and for the first days in the capital city, they slept on the floor in an unfurnished room. "In the night, we would lay our clothes on the floor and sleep on them and early morning we would fold them back into the suitcase," recalls Christine, who recalls times when they could only afford to eat one meal each day.

Nevertheless, the Gumbes persevered. A relentless networker, Sammy pursued his calling by working for and through several global relief organizations. He also served as part-time pastor at Maputo International Christian Fellowship. In June 2001, Sammy and Christine formed what is today Restoration Mission International (RMI). By 2010, Sammy had established a Vision Conference Pastors and Church Leaders Training Program in central Mozambique, preparing dozens of pastors and church leaders of various denominations for effective ministry. "When we came to Mozambique, it was difficult to see how this work could be accomplished, but years later we looked back and realized God had been so faithful to fulfill his purpose in our lives," says Christine.

Sammy passed away in 2011 after battling non-Hodgkin's lymphoma for several months. He was thirty-eight years of age.

I will use a few powerful words to describe Sammy Gumbe. One is "passionate". He had an unstoppable purpose in his life, which was to serve God and to serve his people.

Sammy was also naturally "curious". He was open to almost anybody's idea. He'd listen and be very slow to condemn or throw cold water on what anyone said. I was struck by how many questions he would ask, never talking about himself. He was always asking what others thought about this or that.

Another word is "honest". Sammy's integrity was above reproach. Once after I had sent some money to RMI, I found out that the Gumbe's son was gravely ill. "Just take the money I sent and apply it to your medical bills," I suggested to Sammy. "No," he replied firmly. "I would never take for my own use anything that is sent for ministry." Several times, while traveling with Sammy, guards at check points along the road would ask for bribes. Sammy always refused. Instead, he had the ability to connect on a personal level with the guards, so that we always made it through.

Finally, he had the ability to endure joyfully both the ups and the downs of life, even when he didn't know where his next meal would come from. Sammy just believed that, if the sparrows of the sky were watched and cared for, as Jesus says in the Gospel of Matthew, then the God who called him would feed him. If I could say only one thing about him, it would be, "Sammy was joyful."

As a result, when he taught these pastors and church leaders, they listened to Sammy. They were attentive. They respected his passion, his openness, his integrity, and his personal stability, as well as his knowledge of the scriptures. Sammy was an incredible communicator, and he built up a generation of leaders for the church in Mozambique.

CONTRASTING AND COMPARING THE TWO

Sammy was a black pastor. Andrew is white businessman, though totally African in the sense that he was born and has lived his entire life there. Andrew came from missionary parents, and Sammy came from a family well-connected in Mozambican society and government. So in that sense, they were really culturally different.

But both Sammy and Andrew had an unusually deep love for people—generated by their allegiance to a higher purpose. Both gave up privilege to serve something bigger than themselves, something in which they passionately believed. Sammy felt a real burden for the people of his native Mozambique, and Andrew had an enormous burden for the people around him, to bring them the light and the love of God, and to improve their lives in the process. People gravitate to Andrew. He is the least status-conscious and the most non-authoritarian person I know. Sammy was and Andrew is extremely humble. Both have exhibited fierce resolve.

In his landmark work *Good to Great*, Jim Collins observes that the best leaders "build enduring greatness through a paradoxical blend of personal humility and professional will." He calls this Level 5 Leadership. The best leaders display the tenaciousness of a junkyard dog fighting over a bone, as they pursue their organizational objectives. When things go well, they give credit to others. When it comes to assessing blame, they look in the mirror.

Sammy Gumbe and Andrew Cunningham are two of my exemplars of Level 5 transformational leaders with high **DICE + 1**.

Who exemplifies hope in your life? Will you give hope to others by leading transformationally?

QUICK REFERENCE:
The 4-R Model of Transformational Leadership

AN OUTLINE OF THE 4-R MODEL

Relationships

- *Dynamic Determination*
- *Intellectual Flexibility*
- *Courageous Character*
- *Emotional Maturity*

DICE + 1 (Collaborative Quotient)

Key Point: The stronger your **DICE**, the greater will be your ability to collaborate.

Roles

- *Direction Setter*
- *Spokesperson*
- *Coach*
- *Change Agent*

Key Point: You must play each role well in order to be effective.

Responsibilities

- *Vision-Casting*
- *Strategy-Making*
- *Aligning*
- *Encouraging*

Key Point: All four work together. Vision-Casting generates momentum. Strategy-Making organizes a framework for momentum. Aligning releases momentum into that framework. Encouraging sustains the momentum.

Results

Key Point: It takes a collective effort over time to get important things accomplished. If you are not getting the outcomes you want, use The 4-R Model as a diagnostic tool. Monitor, evaluate, and make adjustments.

QUICK REFERENCE
The 4-R Model of Transformational Leadership

AN OVERVIEW OF THE 4-R MODEL

The 4-R Model offers a simple, visual form for grasping effective leadership. The four Rs of this model remind us that sustainable leadership is driven by personal virtue *(Relationships)* and enhanced by organizational culture *(Roles)*. Required leadership behaviors *(Responsibilities)* are a collaborative practice—not just the concern of leaders but their followers as well. Finally, the *Results* process keeps the team or organization tuned in to reality.

The Relationships category of the model folds the virtues essential to personal leadership capacity into four traits—*Dynamic Determination*, *Intellectual Flexibility*, *Courageous Character*, and *Emotional Maturity*—which determine a leader's *Collaborative Quotient*. Collectively referred to as **DICE + 1**, these are the basic building blocks without which effective transformational leadership is unlikely, if not impossible. These traits represent what all leaders must possess, not what some leaders might possess. Placing virtue-based Relationships at the core of The 4-R Model counters the notion that "good leaders" are those with strong, charismatic personalities or an extraordinary amount of intelligence and technical skill. Simply put, anyone can lead.

The Roles category of the model employs a powerful mix of organizational titles: *Direction Setter*, *Spokesperson*, *Coach*, and *Change Agent*. These Roles address the culture-shaping work of the leader. The Responsibilities category depicts activities every leader must do as he or she seeks to bring substantive change and lasting benefit to others. These Responsibilities include *Vision-Casting*, *Strategy-Making*, *Aligning* people from the heart, and *Encouraging* them in difficult times.

Finally, the Results category of The 4-R Model highlights the critical connection between performance feedback and sustained effectiveness. Results captures the logic and progression of The 4-R Model. Good things happen over time (Results) when we draw from a fund of virtue (Relationships), collaborate in the work of shaping a healthy organizational culture (Roles), and act in a coordinated manner to bring substantive change in accordance with the purpose, values and mission of a team or organization (Responsibilities).

Acknowledgements

To students in the Bethel University MBA program, as well as Bethel Seminary students, whose practical insight and constructive feedback have greatly enhanced our appreciation for the contemporary relevance of Nehemiah.

To our publisher Dave Aeilts for driving this project forward and providing his invaluable advice. This book would not have been possible without his effort and experience.

To our MBA teaching partner, Jim Green, whose personal example of transformational leadership is an inspiration.

To Dr. David Howard, Professor of Old Testament at Bethel Seminary, who for more than a decade has provided us invaluable historical insight into the life and times of Nehemiah.

Finally, to the authors listed in the Bibliography. Each has added to our appreciation for the critical importance of sound leadership in businesses, non-profit organizations, and beyond. Their research and leadership insight has profoundly shaped our thinking and contributed to our understanding of how leadership works in the real world. We recommend each of these sources to those who seek additional insight on leadership practice.

Mark McCloskey
Jim Louwsma

BIBLIOGRAPHY

Introduction

Burns, James MacGregor. *Leadership*. New York: Harper, 2010.

Huntford, Roland. *Shackleton*. New York: Carroll & Graf, 1999.

Perkins, Dennis N.T. *Leading at the Edge*. New York: AMACOM, 2000.

Preface

Hughes, Robert B., and C. Carl Laney. *Tyndale Concise Bible Commentary*. Wheaton, IL: Tyndale House Publishers, 2001.

Chapter 1

Appelquist, Jeff. *Sacred Ground, Leadership Lessons from Gettysburg and Little Big Horn*. Edina, MN: Beaver Pond Press, 2010.

Cloud, Henry. *Integrity: The Courage to Meet the Demands of Reality*. New York: Harper, 2006.

Hoffer, Eric. *The True Believer*. New York: Harper & Row, 1951.

"Joshua Lawrence Chamberlain." *Civil War Trust*. http://www.civilwar.org/education/history/biographies/joshua-lawrence-chamberlain.html (accessed October 5, 2013).

"Joshua L. Chamberlain." *eHistory Archive*. Ohio State University. History Department home page. http://ehistory.osu.edu/uscw/features/people/bio.cfm?PID=17 (accessed October 5, 2013).

Nanus, Burt. *Visionary Leadership*. San Francisco: Jossey-Bass, 1992.

Sharra, Michael. *The Killer Angels*. New York: Random House, 1974.

Stanford, Barb. "The High Cost of Disengaged Employees." *Gallup Business Journal* http://businessjournal.gallup.com/content/247/the-high-cost-of-disengaged-employees.aspx (accessed March 6, 2013).

Chapter 2

Belmonte, Kevin. *William Wilberforce: A Hero for Humanity*. Grand Rapids, MI: Zondervan, 2007.

Metaxas, Eric. *Amazing Grace: William Wilberforce and the Heroic Campaign to End Slavery*. New York: HarperOne, 2007.

Chapter 3

Block, Gay, and Malka Brucker. *Rescuers: Portraits of Moral Courage in the Holocaust.* New York: Holmes & Meier, 1992.

Bradford, Sarah. *Harriet Tubman: The Moses of Her People.* Mineola, NY: Dover Publications, 2004.

Carrol, J. *Constantine's Sword - The Church and the Jews, A History.* New York: Houghton Mifflin Company, 2001.

Clinton, Catherine. *Harriet Tubman: The Road to Freedom.* New York: Back Bay Books, 2005.

Cloud, Henry. *Integrity: The Courage to Meet the Demands of Reality.* New York: Harper, 2006.

Covey, Stephen R. *The 7 Habits of Highly Effective People.* New York: Simon & Schuster, 2004.

Eliot, George. *Middlemarch.* New York: Penguin Classics, 2007.

"Ellen Johnson Sirleaf.biography." *Bio. True Story (A&E Networks),* http://www.biography.com/people/ellen-johnson-sirleaf-201269 (accessed November 16, 2013).

"Ellen Johnson Sirleaf–Facts." *Nobelprize.org.* Nobel Media AB 2013. http://www.nobelprize.org/nobel_prizes/peace/laureates/2011/johnson_sirleaf-facts.html (accessed February 4, 2014).

Glad, B. and R. Blanton, "F.W. de Klerk and Nelson Mandela: A Study in Cooperative Transformational Leadership." *Presidential Studies Quarterly* 27 (June 1997): 565-590.

Goodwin, Doris Kearns. *Team of Rivals: The Political Genius of Abraham Lincoln.* New York: Simon & Schuster, 2006.

Israel, Adrienne. *Amanda Berry Smith.* Lanham, MD: Scarecrow Press, 1998.

Larson, Kate Clifford. *Bound for the Promised Land: Harriet Tubman: Portrait of an American Hero.* New York: One World, 2004.

Mandela, Nelson. *Long Walk to Freedom.* New York: Little, Brown and Company, 1994.

Royal, Robert. *The Catholic Martyrs of the Twentieth Century - A Comprehensive World History.* New York: The Crossroad Publishing Company, 2000.

Sampson, Anthony. *Mandela: The Authorized Biography*. New York: Vintage Books, 2000.

Sirleaf, Ellen Johnson, *This Child Will Be Great: Memoir of a Remarkable Life by Africa's First Woman President*. New York: HarperCollins, 2009.

Smith, Amanda Berry. *An Autobiography: The Story of the Lord's Dealings with Mrs. Amanda Smith, the Colored Evangelist*. Chicago: Meyer & Brother Publishers, 1893.

Tec, Nachama. *When Light Pierced the Darkness: Christians Rescue Jews in Nazi-Occupied Poland*. New York: Oxford Press, 1986.

Wall Street. Dir. Oliver Stone. Perf. Charlie Sheen, Michael Douglas, Darryl Hannah, Martin Sheen. Screenplay by Stone and Stanley Weiser. 20th Century Fox, 1987.

Chapter 4

Churchill, Winston S. *The World Crisis*. New York: Charles Scribner's Sons, 1923.

Collins, Jim C., and Jerry I. Porras. *Built to Last: Successful Habits of Visionary Companies*. New York: HarperBusiness, 2004.

Greenwald, John. "Inside the Ford/Firestone Fight." *Time Magazine*, May 29, 2001 http://www.time.com/time/business/article/0,8599,128198,00.html (accessed June 12, 2013).

Ingrassia, Paul. *Crash Course, the American Automobile Industry's Road from Glory to Disaster*. New York: Random House, 2010.

Leggett, Christopher. "The Ford Pinto Case: The Valuation of Life as It Applies to the Negligence-Efficiency Argument." Law & Valuation, Professor Palmiter. Wake Forest University, Winston-Salem, NC. Spring, 1999.

Lutz, Bob. *Car Guys vs. Bean Counters, the Battle for the Soul of American Business*. New York: Penguin Group, 2011.

Manchester, William. *The Last Lion*. New York: Little, Brown and Company, 1983.

Maxwell, John. *The 21 Irrefutable Laws of Leadership: Follow Them and People Will Follow You*. Nashville, TN: Thomas Nelson, 2007.

"Our Credo Values." Johnson & Johnson. http://www.jnj.com/connect/about-jnj/jnj-credo (accessed March 18, 2012).

Sonnenfeld, Jeffrey A. "How Rick Waggoner Lost GM." *Bloomberg*

Businessweek, June 1, 2009.

Stelter, Nicole. "Definition of Workplace Culture." *eHow Money*. http://www.ehow.com/facts_5768486_definition-workplace-culture.html (accessed May 14, 2013).

Susi, Reyna. "Effective Crisis Management: Tylenol Scandal 1982." *Interactive Media Lab*. University of Florida. http://iml.jou.ufl.edu/projects/fall02/susi/tylenol.htm (accessed March 12, 2013).

Ten Berge, Diedonnée. *The First 24 Hours: A Comprehensive Guide to Successful Crisis Communications*. Cambridge, MA: Basil Blackwell, 1990.

Terraine, John. *Douglas Haig: The Educated Soldier*. London: Hutchinson Press, 1963.

Wilde, Kevin D. "Leadership Recipe: We Refine it at General Mills." *Leadership Excellence*. November 2012.

Womack, James P., Daniel T. Jones, and Daniel Roos. *The Machine that Changed the World*. New York: Free Press, 1990.

Chapter 5

Fell, Jason and the Entrepreneur Staff. "Steve Jobs: An Extraordinary Career." *Entrepeneur.com*. http://www.entrepreneur.com/article/197538 (accessed April 3, 2013).

Isaacson, Walter. *Steve Jobs*. New York: Simon & Schuster, 2011.

Kotter, John P. *Leading Change*. Boston: Harvard Business School Press, 1996.

Lashinsky, Adam. "Boeing Bets Big on the 707." *Greatest Business Decisions of All Time: How Apple, Ford, IBM, Zappos and others made radical choices that changed the course of business*, ed. Verne Harnish. New York: Fortune Books, 2012.

Usborne, David. "The Moment It All Went Wrong for Kodak." *The Independent*. Posted February 20, 2012. http://www.independent.co.uk/news/business/analysis-and-features/the-moment-it-all-went-wrong-for-kodak-6292212.html (accessed April 3, 2013).

Chapter 6

Bazeman, Marx H., and Dolly Chugh. "Decisions Without Borders." *Harvard Business Review*, January 2006.

Block, Peter. *Stewardship: Choosing Service Over Self-Interest*. San Francisco: Berrett-Koehler Publishers, 1993.

"Company History." Buffalo Wild Wings. http://www.buffalowildwings.com/Global/company%20History%20%2029%2012%20Final.pdf (accessed April 12, 2013).

"Dennis Kozlowski.biography." *Biography.com*. http://www.biography.com/people/dennis-kozlowski-234610 (accessed August 23, 2013).

"Things Leaders Do." *Fast Company Magazine*. http://www.fastcompany.com/48877/things-leaders-do (accessed May 18, 2013).

Schorn, Daniel. "Dennis Kozlowski: Prisoner 05A4820." *60 Minutes: CBS News. February 11, 2009*. http://www.cbsnews.com/stories/2007/03/22/60minutes/main2596123.shtml (accessed August 23, 2013).

Symonds, William C. and Pamela L. Moore. "The Most Aggressive CEO." *Businessweek*, May 28, 2001. www.businessweek.com/stories/2001-05-27/the-most-aggressive-ceo (accessed August 23, 2013).

Ulrich, Dave, Jack Zenger, and Norm Smallwood. *Results-Based Leadership*. Boston: Harvard Business School Press, 1999.

Wong, Grace. "Kozlowski Gets Up to 25 Years." *CNNMoney*, September 19, 2005. http://money.cnn.com/2005/09/19/news/newsmakers/kozlowski_sentence/?iid=EL (accessed August 24, 2014).

Chapter 7

The Epilogue

Collins, Jim C. *Good to Great: Why Some Companies Make the Leap and Others Don't*. New York: HarperCollins, 2001.

ABOUT THE AUTHORS

Mark McCloskey

Mark is a graduate of Miami University (BA) and Bethel Seminary, Minnesota (MDiv). He earned his PhD at the University of South Florida in the college of Education, Department of Leadership Development. His focus of study was organizational leadership, adult education, and research and measurement.

Mark returned to Bethel Seminary in 1998 to serve as dean of the Center for Transformational Leadership. He is presently lead faculty for the Master of Arts in Transformational Leadership and Professor of Ministry Leadership. Mark teaches in this program as well as the MBA program at Bethel. Mark has served on the boards of the Christian Legal Society and Christian Conciliation Service of Minnesota, and the Governing Board and Board of Directors of the Urban Leadership Academy. He currently serves as a national board member for Love INC. He consults with businesses, churches, and non-profit organizations in the areas of leadership development, strategic planning, and team building.

Mark is married to Dawnelle, and they reside in Arden Hills, Minnesota. They have two grown children.

Jim Louwsma

Jim started his collegiate career at the University of Michigan and graduated from Wheaton College with a BA. After graduation, he enlisted in the U.S. Navy during the Vietnam War and flew attack jets for five years in the regular Navy and another eight years in the Naval Reserves.

He earned an MBA from the University of Utah and began a sales and marketing career with Procter and Gamble, retiring in 2004 after twenty-eight years. In retirement, or refirement as he prefers to call it, Jim started a leadership consulting company with Mark McCloskey.Jim also teaches transformational leadership, with Mark , in Bethel University's MBA program. In addition, Jim is a co-founder and board chairman of Africaworks, a non-profit organization in southern Africa that creates sustainable jobs for the economically disadvantaged.

Jim and Joanne have been married for over forty years and live in Eden Prairie, Minnesota. They have three grown children and five grandchildren. Besides family, Jim's interests include racquetball, biking, hiking, and backpacking.

NOTES

....
....
....
....
....
....
....
....
....
....
....
....
....
....
....
....
....
....
....
....
....
....
....
....
....
....
....
....
....
....

NOTES

NOTES

NOTES

NOTES